Christian Ministry Leaders:

The Barriers that Women

Face in Non-profit

Organizations

Dr. Ona C. Miller

To my personal hidden figures, I appreciate your insight, wisdom, love, prayers, and commitment as women who are valuable to this world and me. You are phenomenal.

Lady Karesa Cooper
Lady Dana Bennett
Lady Tamara Johnson
Lady Beatrice Curry
Lady Ina Miller
Lady Monique Jeffery
Lady Linda Raines
Lady Yumesha Mosley
Lady Alesha Williams
Lady Dorthea Johnigan
Lady Crystal Tolbert

Christian Ministry Leaders: The Barriers that Women Face in Non-profit Organizations

Published by Dr. Ona C. Miller

P.O. Box 181084

Dallas, TX 75218

This book or parts thereof may not be reproduced in any form, stored in retrieval system or transmitted in any form by any means-electronic, mechanical, photocopy, recording or otherwise-without prior written permission of the publisher, except as provided by United States of America copyright law.

Unless otherwise noted, all Scripture quotations are from the King James Version Bible. Scripture quotations marked KJV are from the King James Version of the Bible. Scripture quotations marked NIV are from the Holy Bible, New International Version.

Copyright© 2017, by Dr. Ona C. Miller All rights reserved

ISBN: 978-0-692-84065-8 Printed in the United States of America

Abstract

Despite the need for leadership in Christian ministry, opportunities are often not available to women, because of social, cultural, and perceptual barriers that block their entry into these roles. It was not known how women perceived and overcame social, cultural, and perceptual barriers to succeed as leaders in Christian ministry. The purpose of this qualitative case study was to explore how women perceived and overcame social, cultural, and perceptual barriers to succeed as leaders in Christian ministry. Servant and inclusive leadership theories guided the study. The study's sample consisted of 10 purposively selected females that occupied leadership roles in Christian ministry, and triangulated data using interviews, a survey, and field notes. Five common themes were uncovered: (a) female perception of leadership (b) characteristics of female leadership (c) internal and external barriers (d) leadership momentum (e) coping mechanisms. According to servant leadership and inclusive leadership theory, it is every individual leader's purpose to serve others in a selfless fashion. Servant leadership and inclusive leadership theory, it is every individual leader's purpose to serve others in a selfless fashion. Serving others is inclusive of all and is not limited to perception or certain groups. Serving others is selfless, but turns into selfishness when leadership intentionally and purposefully employs external obstructions of biases and discrimination.

Keywords: Servant Leadership, Inclusive Leadership, Women in Leadership, Female Christian Ministry Leaders, Internal Barriers, External Barriers, Coping Mechanisms, Female Perceptions of leadership, Leadership Career Momentum

Dedication

I dedicate this study to every female and female leader. Life has not and does not always render fairness. Nevertheless, we keep preserving in the midst of challenges. It was our innate ability and character to birth and bring things forth; because of this, we also encounter great distress. However, it was in our distress we always find a way to give life and live life. We sacrifice to serve others willingly, but services are not always reciprocated. Nonetheless, I have never experienced God forsake us and I am certain that He never will.

Acknowledgments

I would like to acknowledge my family who has been by my side every step of the way. I appreciate my mother, Kaye Frances Fry Miller, who is the educator and teacher of 43 years. She taught me everything there was to know about being a woman in this world. I express gratefulness to my father, Afanual Miller, Jr., who consistently gave me the unconditional love and support any daughter would desire. I extend much love to my sister, Ina Keturah Miller, who stands beside me in everything that I do. We were raised always to stick together, no matter what. She is my friend, pal, and sister. She is my older sister that has brains, talent, and beauty. To my nephew, Midian Tyrus-Ishmael Lee, he encourages me to be the example for the world to see. He brings me great joy and priceless memories of his life. Everything that I do, I execute a plan with my family in my mind as my priority. I hope that I make each of you proud. Lastly, to Dr. Adell Newman-Lee, Dr. Nancy Walker, and Dr. Bridgette Anne Sullenger you all were an amazing dissertation committee. Thank you for your relentless support and encouragement. I could not have done this without each of you.

Table of Contents

List of Tables xii

List of Figures xiii

Chapter 1: Introduction to the Study 1

    Introduction 1

    Background of the Study 4

    Problem Statement 7

    Purpose of the Study 9

    Research Questions 11

    Advancing Scientific Knowledge 14

    Significance of the Study 19

    Rationale for Methodology 22

    Nature of the Research Design for the Study 24

    Definition of Terms 34

    Assumptions, Limitations, and Delimitations 38

    Summary and Organization of the Remainder of the Study 43

    Chapter 2: Literature Review 53

Introduction to the Chapter and Background to the
Problem 53
    Theoretical Foundation... 66
    Review of the Literature 75
    Methodology 116
    Instrumentation 118
    Data Collection 120
    Summary 121
Chapter 3: Methodology 126
    Introduction 126
    Statement of the Problem 127
    Research Questions 131
    Research Methodology 137
    Research Design 140
    Population and Sample Selection 143
    Sources of Data 149
    Validity 153
    Reliability 154
    Data Collection and Management 157

Protection and management of data.................. 161

Data Analysis Procedures 164

Ethical Considerations 173

Limitations and Delimitations................................... 176

Summary 179

Chapter 4: Data Analysis and Results 185

Introduction.. 185

Descriptive Data... 187

Data Analysis Procedures 194

    Data analysis approach 195

    Preparation of data... 197

    Analysis of data 200

    Coding using NVivo 203

Results 226

    Internal barriers vs. external barriers 231

    Coping mechanisms 250

    Characteristics of female leadership 265

    Female perception of leadership....................... 274

    Leadership momentum....................................... 287

Summary.. 290

Chapter 5: Summary, Conclusions, and

    Recommendations 292

Introduction 292

Summary of the Study 294

Significance of the Study 300

Summary of Findings and Conclusions 303

Implications 332

    Theoretical implications. 333

    Practical implications. 336

    Future implications 338

Recommendations 341

    Recommendations for future research. 341

    Recommendations for future practice. 344

Conclusions 347

References 351

List of Tables

Table 1. Participants' Demographics 188

Table 2. Participants' Positions in Christian Ministry ... 188

Table 3. Data Summary 191

Table 4. Codes for Female Perceptions of Leadership .. 209

Table 5. Codes for Characteristics of Female Leadership 211

Table 6. Codes for Internal and External Barriers 217

Table 7. Codes for Leadership Career Momentum 219

Table 8. Codes for Coping Mechanisms 221

Table 9. Coping Mechanisms Frequently Mentioned 254

Table 10. Coping Mechanisms 257

Table 11. Inherent and Learned Characteristics 267

Table 12. Perception of Faced Barriers 277

Table 13. Perceptions of Leadership 278

List of Figures

Figure 1. Research procedure. 163

Figure 2. Represents common words and phrases by occurrences per word, phrase, theme, and code. 199

Figure 3. Common themes that emerged from the coded data. 231

Figure 4. Topics of discussion relevant to internal and external barriers. 243

Figure 5. Coping mechanism hierarchies as grouped by hierarchy. 255

Figure 6. Breakdown of theme related to not coping well. 258

Figure 7. Participants' identified inherent characteristics that are attributes of success. 259

Figure 8. Participants' explanations of self-expectations. 259

Figure 9. Comparison of participants' leader and inherent characteristics. 268

Figure 10. Participants' expressions of perceived internal barriers. 280

Figure 11. Participants' explanations of leadership career momentum. 290

Chapter 1: Introduction to the Study

Introduction

The need for leaders in Christian ministry cannot be overemphasized. There is a lack of diversity in female Christian ministry leaders in a non-profit organization. Despite this need for leaders in Christian ministry, the opportunity was not always available to women because social, cultural, and perceptual barriers block their entry into these roles (Virick & Greer, 2012). Christian ministry is a sacrificial service to carry out the commission of God here on earth. Women have taken steps to become capable leaders through education, training, and development to meet the expectations of being a Christian ministry leader. Mento (2014) believes that nonprofit organizations, including those related to Christian ministry, are actually hindered by not having women in leadership roles. Women have innate abilities to nurture growth. Nonprofit organizations like a Christian ministry recognize the need to serve others within the community. This may derive change regardless of constraints presented by society and culture about women (Skelly & Johnson, 2011). Contained in this chapter is a broad overview of female Christian ministry leader's self-perceptions of their experiences and the barriers that they are faced with in attaining and maintaining leadership positions. This chapter began with the background of the study that explained the history, the problem statement that revealed the existing problems, the purpose of the study that defined the intent, and the research questions, which were tools used to gaining the necessary information for this study to be completed. The details of this chapter were followed by the literary review, which was included in Chapter 2. The purpose of this qualitative case study was to explore how women perceived and overcame social, cultural, and perceptual barriers to succeed as leaders in Christian ministry (Scott, 2010). Secondly, to examine what measures women have taken to overcome these barriers Michailidis, Morphitou, & Theophylatou, (2012). Thirdly, identify inherent and learned characteristics necessary for Christian leadership (Wienclaw, 2015). It also identified the inherent and learned characteristics necessary for Christian leadership and the steps women have taken to overcome barriers.

Servant leadership theory provided a base for understanding this phenomenon. Additionally, inclusive leadership provided a prospective that included diverse perceptions, but with the need to find and understand relatable common places to enhance the well-being of individuals, groups, and organizations (Jaworski, 2012). While there was ample literature that explored female Christian ministry leaders, this study examined an area that has been under-represented in literature, i.e., how women perceive the constraints and their own leadership abilities (Johns, 2013).

The remaining chapters in this study continued with Chapter 2. In this study, Chapter 2 entailed the theoretical and conceptual framework, which served as a foundation for this research, as well as an overview of the literature that supported this study. Subsequently was the Chapter 3, which collaborated the design of the study including how and what method it was implemented. Next, Chapter 4 incorporated the data collected, and the results of the study. Finally, In Chapter 5, the researcher translated the findings, drew conclusions, and made recommendations that enhanced future research and leadership.

Background of the Study

Christian ministry has traditionally been dominated by men and social mores have opposed women in these leadership positions (Forbes, 2011). The percentage of women serving in Christian ministry has increased slightly in recent decades; however, there is a disparity among women in leadership in non-profit organizations compared to men (GuideStar, 2011). Women have been underrepresented in leadership within nonprofit organizations for many decades (Rivkin, Diestel, & Schmidt, 2014). Continuing perceptions of these roles as male specific positions have imposed considerable restraints on female Christian ministry leaders. This is primarily due to cultural perceptions, cultural behaviors, and cultural diversity (Paustian-Underdahl, Walker, & Woehr, 2014).

The purpose of this research was to reveal the personal, social, and perceptual barriers that women face when they seek Christian leadership positions (Scott, 2010). Secondly, to examine what measures women have taken to overcome these barriers (Michailidis et al., 2012). Thirdly, identify inherent and learned characteristics necessary for Christian leadership (Wienclaw, 2015). It also identified inherent and learned characteristics necessary for Christian leadership and the steps women have taken to overcome barriers.

Servant leadership theory and inclusive leadership theory provided a base for understanding this phenomenon. Greenleaf (1977) is a foundational author of servant leadership. Servant leadership, according to Greenleaf (1977) is a natural desire of each person, an innate feeling moving one to lead rather than be lead. Thus if servant leadership is innate, then one should be able to perceive it at many levels. Additionally inclusive leadership provided a prospective that included diverse perceptions, but with the need to find and understand relatable common places to enhance the well-being of individuals, groups, and organizations (Jaworski, 2012)

While there was ample literature that explored female Christian ministry leaders, this study examined an area that has been under represented in literature, i.e., how women perceive the constraints and their own leadership abilities. (Johns, 2013). Constraints places limits on the leader, followers, and the overall organization. The ultimate goal for an organization is to be productive and experience growth in the services that are provided and the employees proving the services (Jaworski, 2012). Leaders are the most vital element within an organization to foster, nurture, and cultivate growth. Where there is no growth, constraints are evident.

However, women have continued to seek to enter this field. According to C.E. Washington (2010), female Christian ministry leaders can succeed when equipped with proper training, mentorship, and education. A strategy for success can lead to breakthroughs for women, although remaining perceptions of women as lacking the right qualities for this type of leadership can present areas of discomfort, challenges, and barriers (Nwoye, 2011). The perception of society has slightly loosened its grip on women in Christian ministry as progress has occurred. However, women are still faced with internal and external barriers from a variety of sources (Smith, Crittenden, & Caputi, 2012).

Problem Statement

It was not known how women perceived and overcame social, cultural, and perceptual barriers to succeed as leaders in Christian ministry. Social barriers are created when the normal traditions find it challenging to relate to other beliefs and traditions. Social barriers only exist as reserves people have about other individuals or groups, which usually has no bearing on the people that are victim. Social barriers exist because classes, categories, and biases are created due to appearance or different views. Cultural barriers influence the behaviors, attitudes, and customary practices of how one group views another group or individual. Perceptual barriers are internal barriers of individuals or groups that think differently with beliefs that are not understood or generally accepted (Nwoye, 2011).

Examining female Christian ministry leaders' experiences with internal and external barriers that exist because of the perception of society and culture provided a basis for understanding what these barriers are, and how to negate those barriers (Christian & Zippay, 2012). According to Mento (2014), women in leadership nurture growth, a valuable asset to Christian leadership. This study seeks to understand how women perceive their personal obstacles in Christian leadership. Furthermore, this research revealed the personal, social, and perceptual barriers that women face when they seek Christian leadership positions and what some have done to overcome these barriers. It also identified inherent and learned characteristics necessary for Christian leadership. Therefore, this study provided insight and strategy on these barriers. A strategy was determined as to women in leadership can be successful despite the barriers (Newkirk & Cooper, 2013)

Purpose of the Study

The purpose of this qualitative case study was to explore how women perceived and overcame social, cultural, and perceptual barriers to succeed as leaders in Christian ministry (Ryan, Haslam, Hersby, & Bongiorno, 2011). The internal barriers that exist because of cultural beliefs play a vital role in leadership. The external factors of social interaction were a determining factor in what was deemed acceptable within an organization. However, the greatest challenge that was faced, as a female Christian ministry leader was the self-perceived barriers that exist for women in Christian ministry leadership was examined through direct interaction with the participants (Johnson & Christensen, 2012). The phenomenon to be studied was how women in leadership perceive their experiences as leaders, how they explain their own learned and inherent characteristics, why they persevere in this profession, and how they contend with barriers in Christian ministry within the United States. The results received were synthesized by themes, codes, comparison, and summarization. The target population was 10–15 female Christian ministry leaders within various cities within the United States (Frost, 2011). The population was recruited via purposive methods from among a group of women in Christian leadership positions within the United States, who can be contacted by the researcher and asked to participate.

Stake (1995) recommended a qualitative methodology design as a powerful narrative and investigation of a phenomenon, such as the self-perceived barriers of women in Christian leadership positions. Therefore, a qualitative case study design was used to examine how women in leadership perceive their experiences in Christian ministry. Qualitative case studies provide a deeper understanding of a phenomenon through producing a deeper response to the open-ended interview questions. The case study investigated the strength of the relationship between perceived self-identified inherent and learned characteristics of success (Stake, 1978, 1995, 1998). The qualitative methodology was the best approach for answering the research questions because it examines the barriers, experiences, and self-perceptions that exist for female Christian ministry leaders (Lambert & Lambert, 2012). Understanding this phenomenon was a requirement in gaining access into clarifying the perceptions of the participants. The qualitative methodology is different from numbers, frequencies, and amounts that are involved with quantitative research (Stake, 1995).

Research Questions

The phenomena under investigation by the researcher explored how women in Christian ministry leadership perceive their experiences and contend with internal and external barriers in Christian ministry. The female Christian ministry leaders' experiences revealed obstacles as well as define strategies for success in Christian ministry. Some female Christian ministry Leaders has overcome barriers. Society and culture have trained women to become effective leaders by overcoming these barriers. Female Christian ministry leaders are subject to the reality of biases, favoritism, and discrimination. These barriers are largely present due to cultural perceptions and behaviors. Analyzing the experiences of women in leadership positions identified, and categorized the perception of their experiences. The examination of their experiences identified pathways to improve societal perceptions. The purpose of this qualitative case study was to explore how women perceived and overcame social, cultural, and perceptual barriers to succeed as leaders in Christian ministry (Scott, 2010). Secondly, to examine what measures women have taken to overcome these barriers (Michailidis et al., 2012).

Thirdly, identify the inherent and learned characteristics necessary for Christian leadership (Wienclaw, 2015)

> R1: What social barriers do women face when they seek Christian leadership positions?
>
> R2: What cultural barriers do women face when they seek Christian leadership positions?
>
> R3: What perceptual barriers do women face when they seek Christian leadership positions?
>
> R4: How have women overcome social, cultural, and perceptual barriers when taking on leadership roles in Christian ministry?

Gaining an understanding of how women in Christian leadership identify and perceive social, cultural, and self-perceived barriers, fulfilled the purpose of this study. The purpose of this study was to explore how women perceived and overcame social, cultural, and perceptual barriers to succeed as leaders in Christian ministry. The "how" question, identified the steps that women have successfully taken to overcome current social, cultural, and perceptual barriers. The perceptions of these barriers, regarding this phenomenon remain unknown. Discovering the "what" question identified and provides information unknown regarding the social, cultural, and perceptual barriers that women face when seeking leadership positions. Answering the posed "why" question delves deeper into the phenomenon by expanding on the perseverance of women to overcome barriers, furthering the study, and addressing better the purpose and problem of this study. The qualitative methodology with a case study design makes answering these questions possible by allowing participants to describe in detail, their perceptions, accounts, and experiences with the phenomenon (Yin, 2009).

Advancing Scientific Knowledge

While the percentage for Female Christian Ministry Leaders in nonprofit organizations has increased in recent years (Virick & Greer, 2012), women in leadership within Christian ministry continues to fall significantly short of men in similar positions (Holst & Kirsch, 2015). The opportunities are limited for Female Christian Ministry Leaders and existing negative perceptions prevent women from securing a leadership position. The commitment and confidence in women as leaders remain entrenched in society and culture, which poses internal obstacles for women seeking leadership position in Christian ministry. (Vasavada, 2012). According to a study done on preparing women for leadership in Black Baptist churches, (Newkirk & Cooper, 2013) women who seek out leadership position in Christian ministry must deal with personal issues of sexism, financial struggles and oppression. The study further stated that women in Christian leadership would need to be fully prepared to deal with the common issues affecting churches, which might include spiritual, social, political, and economic issues. Newkirk and Cooper (2013) further found that "women who choose to embark in this profession face challenges and struggles, which their male counterparts often do not experience" (p. 324). As long as these barriers exist, women who seek to become Christian Ministry

Leaders will face obstacles to reaching their goals. By examining the experiences of female Christian ministry, leaders who are or have been affected by external and personal barriers provided a basis for understanding what these barriers are, and how to overcome those barriers (Christian & Zippay, 2012).

This study seeks to understand how women perceive their external and personal obstacles in Christian leadership. Furthermore, this research revealed the social and self-perceptual barriers that women face when they seek Christian leadership positions and what some have done to overcome these barriers. It also identified inherent and learned characteristics necessary for Christian leadership. For instance, according to Mento (2014), women in leadership nurture growth, a valuable asset to Christian leadership. However, this study provided insight on those unique and inherent barriers that women face when seeking leadership roles in Christian ministry. Female specific strategies to success in Christian leadership despite the barriers also are examined (Newkirk & Cooper, 2013).

The foundation of this study was Servant leadership and additionally included was Inclusive leadership; both theories identified the desire of the leader to serve and the need for leaders willing to serve, regardless of culture, society, and perception. Female Christian ministry leaders are inclusive of proving service as a leader to all and should be able to serve without bias, discrimination, or prejudice. Servant leadership theory provided a base for understanding the phenomenon of the barriers that women face in Christian ministry when desiring to serve. Additionally, inclusive leadership also provided a prospective that included diverse individuals, culture, and perceptions, but with the need to find and understand relatable common places to enhance the well-being of individuals, groups, and organizations (Jaworski, 2012).

Because there are some women that have been successful in serving as a leader in Christian ministry despite barriers, the study examined what measures women have taken to overcome social, cultural, and perceptual barriers, which educated future generations of women seeking leadership in Christian ministry (Michailidis et al., 2012). The research questions identified inherent and learned characteristics that are evident due to perceived expectations of society and culture for women seeking leadership positions (Wienclaw, 2015)

While there was ample literature that explored female Christian ministry leaders, this study examined an area that has been under represented in literature, i.e., how women perceive the constraints and their own leadership abilities. (Moor, Cohen, & Beeri, 2015). Exploring the perceptions and experiences of female Christian ministry leader's abilities developed strategies to overcome barriers and attain success. The research of this study extends both theories, because it provided a strategy or strategies that helped female leaders to overcome barriers and be successful in Christian ministry.

Significance of the Study

The significance of this study examined the experiences and perceptions of female Christian ministry leaders and identified what barriers exist because of social, cultural, and their own personal perceptions (Bowles, 2014). This research explored the steps that female Christian ministry leaders have taken to overcome some barriers and discovered a strategy to decrease or eliminate existing barriers in Christian ministry. Women in leadership may possess the necessary education, training, and development to lead within Christian ministry however; they must remove barriers to be successful (Herrera, Duncan, Green, & Skaggs, 2012). This study adds to the current literature by analyzing the respondent's perceptions, regarding internal and external barriers to leadership, steps women have taken to overcome barriers, and why they persevere despite obstacles.

Examining female Christian ministry leaders' experiences with internal and external barriers will provided a basis for understanding what these barriers are, and how to negate those barriers (Christian & Zippay, 2012). This study seeks to understand how women perceive their personal obstacles in Christian leadership. Furthermore, this research revealed the personal, social, and perceptual barriers that women face when they seek Christian leadership positions and what some have done to overcome these barriers. It will also identify inherent and learned characteristics necessary for Christian leadership. Therefore, this study will provide insight and strategy on these barriers. A recommendation will be developed as to how women in leadership can be successful despite the barriers (Newkirk & Cooper, 2013)

The phenomena under investigation by the researcher explored how women in Christian ministry leadership perceive their experiences and contend with internal and external barriers in Christian ministry. Women in leadership contend with internal and external barriers in Christian ministry. The female Christian ministry leaders' experiences revealed obstacles as well as define strategies for success in Christian ministry. Some female Christian ministry leaders have overcome barriers. Society and culture have trained women to become effective leaders by overcoming these barriers. Female Christian ministry leaders are subject to the reality of biases, favoritism, and discrimination. These barriers are largely present due to cultural perceptions and behaviors. Analyzing the experiences of women in leadership identified and categorized the perception of their experiences. The examination of their experiences identified pathways to improve societal perceptions. The purpose of this qualitative case study was to explore how women perceived and overcame social, cultural, and perceptual barriers to succeed as leaders in Christian ministry (Scott, 2010). Secondly, to examine what measures women have taken to overcome these barriers (Michailidis et al., 2012). Thirdly, identify inherent and learned characteristics necessary for Christian leadership (Wienclaw, 2015). This study provided valuable insight for women who are seeking leadership positions in Christian ministry to be successful by identifying unknown barriers. The experiences of female Christian ministry leaders established a strategy to overcome and attain the position they desire.

Rationale for Methodology

Stake (1995) recommended a qualitative methodology as a powerful narrative and investigation of a phenomenon, such as the self-perceived barriers of women in Christian leadership positions. Therefore, a qualitative case study design was used to examine how women in leadership perceive their experiences in Christian ministry. Qualitative case studies provide a deeper understanding of a phenomenon by producing a deeper response to the interview questions. The qualitative case study investigated the strength of the relationship between self-identified inherent and learned characteristics of success (Stake, 1978, 1995, 1998). The qualitative methodology was the best approach for answering the research questions because it examines the barriers, experiences, and self-perceptions that exist for female Christian ministry leaders (Lambert &

Lambert, 2012). Understanding this phenomenon requires the qualitative methodology to delve into participants' perceptions rather than numbers, frequencies, or amounts like that of quantitative research (Singh, 2015). The qualitative case study was chosen because the mixed-method methodology, like quantitative research, fails to focus on the perceptions of participants, thereby did not generate an understanding of the phenomenon (Singh, 2015). Therefore, the qualitative case study methodology was essential to understanding the posed phenomenon.

The qualitative case study design was selected based on the need to examine the history of unique experiences and narrative self-perceptions of women in leadership. Identifying these barriers helped to uncover hindrances to their success while serving as a leader in Christian ministry (Stake, 1998; Yin, 2009; Johnson & Christensen, 2012). The qualitative case study design was chosen so that the researcher can receive data and information from more than one primary data analysis (Frost, 2011). Merriam (2009) explains that research focused on discovery, insight and understanding from the perspectives of those being studied offers the greatest promise of making significant contributions to the knowledge base and practice of education. Qualitative case study research approaches a problem of practice from a holistic perspective in order to gain an in-depth understanding of the situation and its meaning for those involved. The interest is in process rather than outcomes, in context rather than a specific variable, in discovery rather than in conformation. The case study research design was necessary for this study to explore a qualitative phenomenon. A case study answered the "how" and "why" research questions and explained the contemporary events over time that is the phenomenon (Yin, 2009).

Nature of the Research Design for the Study

The nature of the research design was a case study to answer the research questions by allowing participants to describe, in detail, their perceptions, accounts, and experience with the phenomenon (Yin, 2009). The case study design was selected based on the need to examine the history of unique experiences and narrative self-perceptions of women in Christian leadership. A case study design was chosen because it was best for describing in-depth experiences of people, groups, community, and organizations. A case study allows for direct examination and interaction with the participants (Merriam, 2009). Grounded theory is geared toward building a theory from collected data. The case study design was the best choice after researching other design choices. Ethnography describes the many characteristics of a culture with variables to be studied while identifying specific or specific cultures that are affected, which does not allow the researcher to expand upon the experiences of the individual or group. Another choice is the Phenomenology study, describes an experience that is held deeply among individuals and groups. It is an experience that can be described collectively that encompassed experiences of past, present, and future.

Historical design compares the past and present, with the intent to anticipate the effects of the future. However, it is not considered as the best choice for this study. After careful review and consideration for examining the experiences of female Christian ministry leaders in nonprofit organizations and the barriers that are faced, the case study design was a better choice for this study (Klenke, Wallace, & Martin, 2015).

The goal of this qualitative case study was to examine how women in leadership identify and perceive social, cultural, and perceptual barriers in Christian ministry while discovering the steps for women in leadership to overcome these barriers. Additionally, to reveal their perceptions about their own inherent and learned behaviors that exists because of society and culture. The revelation identified provided an understanding of what causes them to be successful. The qualitative case study design was selected based on the need to examine the history of unique experiences and narrative self-perceptions of women in leadership. Detecting these barriers helped to find hindrances to their success while serving as a leader in Christian ministry (Stake, 1995; Yin, 2009; Johnson & Christensen, 2012). The qualitative case study design was chosen so that the researcher can receive data and information from more than one primary data analysis (Frost, 2011). Merriam (2009) explains that research focused on discovery, insight and understanding from the perspectives of those being studied offers the greatest promise of making significant contributions to the knowledge base and practice of education. Qualitative case study research approaches a problem of practice from a holistic perspective in order to gain an in-depth understanding of the situation and its meaning for those involved. The interest is in process rather than outcomes, in context rather than a specific variable, in discovery rather than in conformation. The case study research design was necessary for this study exploring a qualitative phenomenon. A case study answered the "how" and "why" research questions and explains the contemporary events over time that is the phenomenon (Yin, 2009).

A total sample size of 10 was appropriate to comprise a case and reach saturation (Yin, 2009). The case study research design was necessary for this study exploring a qualitative phenomenon. A case study answered the "how," "what," and "why" research questions and explained the contemporary events over time that was the phenomenon (Yin, 2009). Although phenomenological research gains insightful descriptions of how an individual experienced a phenomenon (Pringle, Hendry, & McLafferty, 2011), case studies reflect real-life experiences and provides in-depth data from open-ended interviews making the case study most appropriate (Yin, 2009; Cronin, 2014). A case study was valuable in collecting workable data from a general population to have substantial data that was not one-sided and represents a particular group of participants that match particular characteristics or criteria (Stake, 1998). While other designs were considered, the case study design was most befitting of this research because the intent of this study was to understand Christian ministry leaders and collect a variety of data regarding experiences.

The population consisted of women leaders in Christian ministry within the United States. The sample size was 10 females who are currently working in leadership positions. This qualitative case study requires the researcher to choose the sample (Stake, 1998); strategically choosing the participants provided a thorough understanding of the phenomenon. The instruments that were used to collect the data for the qualitative case study were questionnaires, open-ended interviews, and field notes used only for clarification by researcher during interviews. Permission was given by the female Christian ministry leaders who lead and/or have established a nonprofit organization. The preparation process prior to collecting data was to get approval of participants, and Institutional Review Board (IRB) approval. Along with the approvals (Appendix B), field-test (Appendix J), for the data collection instruments were tested for approval and accuracy. All data were protected by removing all personal identifiable information such as names, emails, dates, and numbers that may reference or cross-reference the participants. The researcher made efforts to avoid biases, personal beliefs, judgments, partiality, impartiality, discrimination, and favoritism.

The population was recruited via purposive methods from among a group of women in Christian leadership positions who can be contacted by the researcher and asked to participate. Stake (1995) recommends a qualitative methodology design as a powerful narrative and investigation of a phenomenon, such as the self-perceived barriers of women in Christian leadership positions. Therefore, qualitative case study design was used to examine how women in leadership perceive their experiences in Christian ministry. Qualitative case studies provide a deeper understanding of a phenomenon through producing a deeper response to the open-ended interview questions. The descriptive case study investigated the strength of the relationship between self-identified inherent and learned characteristics of success (Stake, 1978, 1995, 1998).

The instruments that were used to collect the data for the triangulation of data gleaned for this qualitative case study include information from questionnaires; audio taped open-ended interviews, and field notes (Stake, 1978, 1995, 1998; Yin, 2009). The qualitative methodology with a case study design draws upon specific data to answer research questions (Isaacs, 2014). The questionnaire was structured to ask 10 women in Christian leadership roles a series of open-ended questions related to the barriers that they contend with in Christian ministry. Researcher-written open-ended interview questions and a questionnaire answered the research questions (Stake, 1978, 1995, 1998; Yin, 2009). A field-test on all of the five open-ended interview questions and questionnaire ensured alignment, appropriateness, and validity. The field test was distributed to 5 female Christian ministry leaders that were volunteers separate from the participants chosen for the qualitative research study. The questions administered during the field-test rendered results that either confirmed or denied that the researcher indeed was asking the right questions in order to obtain the right information. Questionnaires, which was also be field-tested and approved by a credible source, returned data on demographics, experience, job duties, training, and educational levels. The open-ended interviews for all research questions were captured on NVIVO 10, which is a system that records the open-ended interview and transcribes the data as well. Open-ended questions were presented for all research questions during an open-ended interview and questionnaire for the participant to provide an in depth response to answer what barriers exist and how their experiences are self-perceived while having the opportunity to elaborate on the answer by providing a comment/explanation.

One important concept of the case study was triangulation. Stake (1995) explains that in a case study using our records "to remind us of the need for triangulation"

(p. 107) is essential for triangulation. In addition, triangulation can be achieved through repetitiveness of data gathered from 3 sources, such as interviews, questionnaires, and journal field notes, which provided a challenge to misconceptions and the need for explanations. The qualitative case study structure includes triangulation. First, the researcher should identify the theory concerning the topic. Secondly, a specific and unique phenomenon was identified, which aids in the selection of research questions. After the research questions have been developed, the researcher collects the data from interviews, questionnaires, and journal field notes (Stake, 1978, 1995, 1998; Yin, 2009). The following steps were to organize the data by placing it in order according to categories, patterns, and themes related to the topic, which allowed for editing (Isaacs, 2014). The researcher then formulated triangulation of interviews, journal field notes, and questionnaires to properly transcribe and interpret (Yin, 2014).

Table 1 links the interview question, questionnaire, and sub questions that formulate the answers to the appropriate research question. The questionnaire was a more generalized open-ended format for participants to express their thoughts in their own words. Once the participant's responses were received, from the questionnaire, then the open-ended interview questions were distributed to the participants. During the interview, additional questions were also asked to gather a deeper sense of what was being said. Both responses from questionnaire and interview were aligned to the appropriate research question.

Definition of Terms

This section provides the critical definitions of terms used throughout the scope of this study. The definitions are provided as a way of ensuring reading comprehension and consistency of the terminology used throughout the study.

Leader. A leader is someone who exercises authority over other people. Leadership entails being in charge of other people in multiple ways. It consists of influencing, motivating, organizing, and coordinating the work of others (Chin & Sanchez-Hucles, 2007).

Christian ministry. Christian ministry is an activity carried out by Christians to express or spread their faith (Ross, 2015). Christian ministry consists of a group of like-minded individuals of same faith, expressing and demonstrating the Great Commission (Ross, 2015).

Non-profit organization. A Nonprofit organization is a special type of corporation that has been organized to meet specific tax-exempt purposes such as a religious organization, charitable organization, or political organization (Duncan & Schoor, 2015).

Servant leadership. Servant-leadership is a theoretical framework that advocates a leader's primary motivation and role as service to others (Greenleaf, 1977).

Inclusive leadership. Inclusive leadership is the practice of leadership that carefully includes the contributions of all stakeholders in the community or organization. Inclusion means being at the table at all levels of the organization, being a valued contributor and being fully responsible for your contribution to the ultimate result (Fierke, Lui, Lepp, & Baldwin, 2014).

Barriers. Circumstances or obstacles that keep people and things apart and prevent communication or progress. Barriers can exist in many different forms, such as mental, emotional, psychological, and physical. Barriers identified and existing barriers can be placed in 2 categories, internal and external. (Newkirk & Cooper, 2013).

Self-perception. The way in which and individual internally views and perceives themselves. Self-Perception includes our internal thoughts and feelings that are expressed outwardly in our actions. (Lambert & Lambert, 2012).

Experiences. A practical contact with and observation of facts or events, encounter or undergo of an event or occurrence (Bryant-Anderson & Roby, 2012).

Leadership theory. A leadership theory is an assumption about distinguishing characteristics of a particular kind of leader. Theories focus on determining specific qualities, such as skill levels, that separate a leader from a follower (Dahlvig & Longman, 2010).

Ethical leadership. Ethical leadership is leadership that is directed by respect for ethical beliefs and values and for the dignity and rights of others. It is thus related to concepts such as trust, honesty, consideration, charisma and fairness (Taylor & Pattie, 2014).

The phenomenon is how women in leadership perceive their experiences in Christian ministry. Women in leadership contend with internal and external barriers in Christian ministry. The female Christian ministry leaders' experiences revealed obstacles as well as helped defined strategies for success in Christian ministry. Some female Christian ministry leaders have overcome barriers. Society and culture have trained women to become effective leaders by overcoming these barriers. Female Christian ministry leaders are subject to the reality of biases, favoritism, and discrimination. These barriers are largely present due to cultural perceptions and behaviors. Analyzing the experiences of women in leadership positions identified and categorized the perception of their experiences. The examination of their experiences identified pathways to improve societal perceptions. The purpose of this qualitative case study was to explore how women perceived and overcame social, cultural, and perceptual barriers to succeed as leaders in Christian ministry (Scott, 2010). Secondly, to examine what measures women have taken to overcome these barriers (Michailidis et al., 2012). Thirdly, identify inherent and learned characteristics necessary for Christian leadership (Wienclaw, 2015)

Assumptions, Limitations, and Delimitations

One assumption related to this qualitative case study was that participants would respond to interview questions with true, honest, and open method in the face-to-face interview sessions. The assumption was that participants would accurately reflect on the accounts and considerations regarding the perception of their experiences. That was a concern in qualitative case studies since participants would be self-reporting experiences when answering the questionnaires and interview questions (Yin, 2009). Through self-reflection, the participants shared their self-perceptions regarding their leadership experiences as women in Christian ministry. Another assumption would be that the participants would be able to control their emotions, feelings, thoughts, and actions by channeling them in a way that was conducive to capturing their true thoughts. In addition, the participants would allow the self-reflection interview time to reveal thoughts, ideas, themes that have never been spoken, but have always been a thought, whether in the forefront or back of their mind. During the interview, the participants would have times of self-reflection on the experiences and the self-reactions or self-responses that were influenced by certain external factors. Therefore, it was assumed that the participant's responses would generate the necessary information to identify barriers that influence female Christian ministry leaders. Self-reactions and self-responses would identify behaviors of the participants, which provided crucial information regarding their perception of the experiences.

There were also limitations based on the study's methodology, research design, and processes of data collection and analysis. In this qualitative case study, one limitation was the accuracy of participants' responses, as participants were self-reporting on their experiences (Yin, 2009). The limitations of this qualitative case study are the participants of the sample size of 10 female Christian ministry leaders who were willing to reflect on their experiences and give accurate details to the encounter.

One limitation was being dependent upon non-numerical data. Secondly, another limitation of a qualitative case study was the flexibility. The researcher has the flexibility to determine the appropriate questions, but if the inappropriate question was asked, the participant may provide unwanted calculations of their experiences, which has the probability of skewing the desired results. Thirdly, the described experiences could very well be painful or something that the participant was not ready to face and the participant could become offended or defensive. The fourth limitation was accurate memory regarding the experiences and describing old feelings that have been covered or previously dealt with. The participants were able to give accounts of their experiences, but there could be limitations of distorted perceptions. Lastly, the limitations of personal assumptions by the researcher, because there is an understanding that barriers do exist for female Christian ministry leaders.

Delimitations include the chosen participants of the study, as each participant was a female Christian ministry leader, of a nonprofit organization, and has had or was having life experiences of the phenomenon to share in the interview. Because the female Christian ministry leaders are still experiences some barriers the researcher must be sensitive to the nature of the study and provide ways of comfort. The researcher kept a jovial disposition with a smile during the interview process. The researcher brought out elements of learning through the shared experiences and identified ways that it has strengthened the participants. Although the participants may have felt sad and shed, some tears the researcher reminded them of how far they have come and the growth that was evident. Another, delimitation to the study was the location of the participants. The 10 participants chosen to participate in the research study were female Christian ministry leaders in various types of non-profit organizations in different cities and states.

    Delimitations were also based on what the researcher did not do during the study. The researcher did not pass judgment or pretend to know exactly how the participant felt. However, the researcher attempted to understand and identify as a woman, as a leader with the current societal and cultural barriers. The literature reviewed for this study pertained to the barriers that women face as a female leader in Christian ministry in a non-profit organization. The phenomenon that was studied was how women in leadership perceived their experiences as leaders, how they explained their own learned and inherent characteristics, why they persevered in the profession, and how they contended with barriers in Christian ministry within the United States. Other research topics were excluded to avoid clouding the focus of the study. The researcher did not use previously constructed interviews or questionnaires, as these data collection methods were not designed for the same purpose of the study.

Summary and Organization of the Remainder of the Study

Christian ministry has traditionally been dominated by men and social mores have opposed women in these leadership positions (Forbes, 2011). The percentage of women serving in Christian ministry has increased slightly in recent decades however; there was a disparity among women in leadership in non-profit organizations compared to men (GuideStar, 2011). Women have been underrepresented in leadership within nonprofit organizations for many decades (Rivkin et al., 2014).

Continuing perceptions of these roles as male specific positions have imposed considerable restraints on female Christian ministry leaders. This was primarily due to cultural perceptions, cultural behaviors, and cultural diversity (Paustian-Underdahl et al., 2014).

However, women continue to seek to enter this field. According to C.E. Washington (2010), female Christian ministry leaders can succeed when equipped with proper training, mentorship, and education. A strategy for success can lead to breakthroughs for women, although the remaining perceptions of women as lacking the right qualities for this type of leadership can present areas of discomfort, challenges, and barriers (Nwoye, 2011). The perception of society has slightly loosened its grip on women in Christian ministry as progress has occurred. However, women are still faced with internal and external barriers from a variety of sources (Smith et al., 2012).

In 1977, Greenleaf's Servant leadership theory proposed a model based primarily on helping others to grow as individuals and within the community (Kemp, 2016). Servant leadership was important to this study because it serving others is not gender specific and provides a foundational standard for female Christian ministry leader to serve others regardless of gender barriers (Berger, 2014). The researcher examined the personal, social, and perceptual barriers that female Christian ministry leaders face in Christian ministry. It also identified inherent and learned characteristics necessary for Christian leadership. Servant leadership theory provided a base for understanding this phenomenon. Additionally, inclusive leadership also provided a prospective that included diverse perceptions, but with the need to find and understand relatable common places to enhance the well-being of individuals, groups, and organizations (Jaworski, 2012). Inclusive leadership was important to female Christian ministry leaders because there was a need to find a common place and remove barriers (Tidball, 2012). Inclusive leadership comprehends the need for diverse cultures and promotes ways to increase acceptance while broadening perspectives. Inclusive leadership distributes power and mutual respect so that one group or individual was not in total control (Beaty & Davis, 2012).

It was not known how women perceived and overcame social, cultural, and perceptual barriers to succeed as leaders in Christian ministry. Examining female Christian ministry leaders' experiences with internal and external barriers provided a basis for understanding what these barriers are, and how to negate those barriers (Christian & Zippay, 2012). According to Mento (2014), women in leadership nurture growth, a valuable asset to Christian leadership. This study seeks to understand how women perceive their personal obstacles in Christian leadership. Furthermore, this research revealed the personal, social, and perceptual barriers that women face when they seek Christian leadership positions and what some have done to overcome these barriers. It also identified inherent and learned characteristics necessary for Christian leadership.

Therefore, this study provided insight and strategy on these barriers. A strategy was determined whether women in leadership can be successful despite the barriers (Newkirk & Cooper, 2013).

Stake (1995) recommends a qualitative methodology design as a powerful narrative and investigation of a phenomenon, such as the self-perceived barriers of women in Christian leadership positions. Therefore, case study design was used to examine how women in leadership perceive their experiences in Christian ministry. Female Christian ministry leaders in the United States are becoming a sustainable element to leadership of nonprofit organizations (Fiedler, 2010).

The goal of this qualitative study was to examine how women in leadership identify and perceive barriers in Christian ministry and what are the steps for women in leadership to overcome barriers in Christian ministry as well as reveal their perceptions about their own leadership qualities and provide an understanding of what causes them to persevere in this profession. The qualitative case study design was selected based on the need to examine the history of unique experiences and narrative self-perceptions of women in leadership. Identifying these barriers removed hindrances to their success while serving as a leader in Christian ministry (Johnson & Christensen, 2012).

The phenomenon that was studied was how women in leadership perceived their experiences as leaders, how they explained their own learned and inherent characteristics, why they persevered in this profession, and how they contended with barriers in Christian ministry within the United States. The instruments that were used to collect the data for the qualitative case study were questionnaires, interviews, and journal field notes. The qualitative methodology with a case study design drew on specific data to answer research questions (Isaacs, 2014). The questionnaire was structured to ask 10–15 women in Christian leadership roles a series of open-ended questions related to the barriers that they contended within Christian ministry. Researcher-written interview questions and a questionnaire answered the research questions. A field-test on the interview questions and questionnaire ensured alignment, appropriateness, and validity. Questionnaires returned data on demographics, experience, job duties, training, and educational levels. The interviews were captured on NVIVO, which was a system that recorded the interview and transcribed the data as well.

Chapter 2 was organized into four sections including: introduction and background, theoretical foundations, review of the literature, and summary. The theoretical foundations section elaborated on the theories that were used to guide this study. Meanwhile, the purpose of the literature review was to reveal the personal, social, and perceptual barriers that women face when they seek Christian leadership positions (Scott, 2010). Secondly, to examine what measures women have taken to overcome these barriers (Michailidis et al., 2012). Thirdly, identify inherent and learned characteristics necessary for Christian leadership

(Wienclaw, 2015). It also identified inherent and learned characteristics necessary for Christian leadership and the steps women have taken to overcome barriers.

This literature review included information pertaining to cultural perception of women and how historically, gender has played a pivotal role in whether or not women receive Christian Ministry Leadership positions. The societal perception of women has been passed down through cultural teachings while misrepresenting female Christian ministry leaders (Vasavada, 2012). Women in leadership have not always been accepted due to tradition and cultural perceptions, regardless women should not eliminate their leadership assignments. (Bacha & Walker, 2013). Additionally, there was a discussion regarding the cultural behaviors of women in various leadership positions who have learned to adapt and adopt many of the cultural perceptions. Their behaviors have also challenged the set traditions and rituals by going beyond the norm and reaching for what they are purposed to do (Paustian-Underdahl et al.,

2014). Inclusive of cultural perception and cultural behaviors, a continued discussion of cultural barriers examined a training tool for women in leadership to gain knowledge and influence in Christian ministry (Vevere, 2014). Gender diversity in leadership examined female Christian ministry leaders who are influencing the nature of diversity and women in leadership who are fostering relationships between diversity, Christian ministry, and society (Virick & Greer, 2012). Gender differences within certain organization are classified by a variety of metaphors, that signify biases and discriminatory obstacles that hinder women in leadership (Smith et al., 2012). Chapter 2 also identified gaps within the literature and concluded with a comprehensive summary and introduction leading in to Chapter 3 on methodology.

The remainder of this dissertation was organized into three chapters. Chapter 3, Methodology, reviewed the purpose of the study, and communicated the procedures that were used to conduct the research, and analyze the data.

Chapter 4, Data Analysis and Results, will provide the descriptive data, data analysis procedures, and results of the study. Lastly, Chapter 5, Summary, Conclusions, and Recommendations, provided a summary of the study, a summary of the findings and conclusions, implications, and recommendations from the study. References and appendices followed the completion of Chapter 5.

Chapter 2: Literature Review

Introduction to the Chapter and Background to the Problem:

This chapter presents a review of literature regarding the female Christian ministry leader's self-perceptions of their experiences and the barriers that women in leadership have faced in their positions. The barriers that were presented are supported by cultural behavior, cultural perspective, and cultural diversity. This chapter included a substantial amount of research completed in regards to women in leadership; however, the literatures to date, reveals no definite study on the barriers that female Christian ministry leader's face.

Therefore, to be able to identify these barriers, the researcher went deeper into the literature that introduced the topic of female Christian ministry leaders to determine what barriers exist; and, if they exist, how do they enhance the perception of female Christian ministry leaders. Research in multiple academic databases yielded information regarding the phenomena discussing the barriers and self-perceptions that women in leadership contend with, specifically in Christian ministry. The researcher was able to access a minimum of 50 scholarly peer-reviewed, full text articles from an extensive variety of academic areas. The academic areas include EBSCO, ProQuest, and ERIC. Also included are reports from Forbes and GuideStar, which provided information for nonprofit organizations. Seventy-five percent of all references are scholarly sources within the last 5 years and avoids overuse of books and dissertations. The scholarly peer-reviewed, full text articles search terms encapsulated the subjects of Christian ministry, leadership, women in leadership, barriers that women face in leadership, glass ceiling, servant leadership, inclusive leadership, and leadership theories and practices. The information was extrapolated to establish a foundation for this study and provide relevant pieces of information. The pieces of information provided validity that social, culture, and perceptive barriers do exist. Furthermore, during the research and extrapolation process a gap was found and noted.

It was not known how women perceived and overcame social, cultural, and perceptual barriers to succeed as leaders in Christian ministry. The purpose of this qualitative case study was to explore how women perceived and overcame social, cultural, and perceptual barriers to succeed as leaders in Christian ministry. The overall review examined the phenomenon of how women in leadership perceived their experiences as leaders, how they explained their own learned and inherent characteristics, why they persevered in the profession, and how they contended with barriers in Christian ministry. In addition, the researcher reviewed methodical text written by theorists applied in this study on servant leadership. Barriers are subjects or objects that block advancement, such as culture, perceptions, and behaviors. Women contend with these barriers as leaders in Christian ministry.

The study was centered on two relevant themes, to determine the barriers of female Christian ministry leaders: (a) reveal the cultural, social, and perceptual barriers that women face when they seek Christian leadership positions, (b) examine what measures women have taken to overcome these barriers and be successful. Being successful does not mean that female Christian ministry leaders will not face barriers. However, how women respond to those barriers will aid in continued success.

The expansive outline of the research presented in Chapter 1 specified that women in leadership are relevant to Christian ministry and there was a need to identify the existing barriers and self-perceptions of female Christian ministry leaders. Firstly, the review revealed the historical background regarding the personal, social, and perceptual barriers that women face when they seek Christian leadership positions. Secondly, the review examined the existing barriers to see how it affects female Christian ministry leaders and what measures women have taken to overcome these barriers. Thirdly, identify the inherent and learned characteristics necessary for Christian leadership. Finally, the Chapter delved into the literature relating to the phenomenon.

Christian ministry has traditionally been dominated by men and social mores have opposed women in these leadership positions (Forbes, 2011). The percentage of women serving in Christian ministry has increased slightly in recent decades however; there was a disparity among women in leadership in non-profit organizations compared to men (GuideStar, 2011). Women have been underrepresented in leadership within nonprofit organizations for many decades (Rivkin et al., 2014). Continued perceptions of these roles as male specific positions have imposed considerable restraints on female Christian ministry leaders. This was primarily due to cultural perceptions, cultural behaviors, and cultural diversity (Paustian-Underdahl et al., 2014). The purpose of this qualitative case study was to explore how women perceived and overcame social, cultural, and perceptual barriers to succeed as leaders in Christian ministry (Scott, 2010). Secondly, to examine what measures women have taken to overcome these barriers (Michailidis et al., 2012). Thirdly, identify inherent and learned characteristics necessary for Christian leadership (Wienclaw, 2015). It identified inherent and learned characteristics necessary for Christian leadership and the steps women have taken to overcome barriers.

Servant leadership theory and inclusive leadership theory provided a base for understanding this phenomenon. Greenleaf (1977) is a foundational author of servant leadership. Servant leadership, according to Greenleaf (1977), it is a natural desire of each person, an innate feeling moving one to lead rather than be lead. Thus if servant leadership is innate, then one should be able to perceive it at many levels. Additionally, inclusive leadership provided a prospective that included diverse perceptions, but with the need to find and understand relatable common places to enhance the well-being of individuals, groups, and organizations (Jaworski, 2012)

While there was ample literature that explored female Christian ministry leaders, this study examined an area that has been under represented in literature, i.e., how women perceive the constraints and their own leadership abilities. Perception initiates an individual's behavior. A false perception can produce unwarranted outcomes. (Johns, 2013).

However, women continue to seek to enter this field. According to C.E. Washington (2010), female Christian ministry leaders can succeed when equipped with proper training, mentorship, and education. A strategy for success can lead to breakthroughs for women, although the remaining perceptions of women as lacking the right qualities for this type of leadership can present areas of discomfort, challenges, and barriers (Nwoye, 2011). The perception of society has slightly loosened its grip on women in Christian ministry as progress has occurred. However, women are still faced with internal and external barriers from a variety of sources (Smith et al., 2012).

Christian ministry has traditionally been dominated by men and social mores have opposed women in these leadership positions (Forbes, 2011). The percentage of women serving in Christian ministry has increased slightly in recent decades however; there was a disparity among women in leadership in non-profit organizations compared to men (GuideStar, 2011). Women have been underrepresented in leadership within nonprofit organizations for many decades (Rivkin et al., 2014). Continuing perceptions of these roles as male specific positions have imposed considerable restraints on female Christian ministry leaders. This was primarily due to cultural perceptions, cultural behaviors, and cultural diversity (Paustian-Underdahl et al., 2014). The purpose of this qualitative case study was to explore how women perceived and overcame social, cultural, and perceptual barriers to succeed as leaders in Christian ministry (Scott, 2010).

Secondly, to examine what measures women have taken to overcome these barriers (Michailidis et al., 2012). Thirdly, identify inherent and learned characteristics necessary for Christian leadership (Wienclaw, 2015). It identified inherent and learned characteristics necessary for Christian leadership and the steps women have taken to overcome barriers.

Scott (2010) argued that the perceptions of a leader and the perceptions of a woman do not always agree. The perception of a female Christian ministry leader can be both perceived as a good leader and a good woman, but was not always done. History has contended that women did not possess the qualifications or characteristics to lead (McBride, 2011). Society and culture opposed women being assertive enough to be in a leadership positions (Ochoa, 2011). However, according to C.E. Washington (2010), female Christian ministry leaders can succeed when equipped with proper training, mentorship, and education. Women have the knowledge, skills, and ability to be a leader in Christian ministry. Christian ministry has traditionally been dominated by men and social mores have opposed women in these leadership positions (Forbes, 2011). The percentage of women serving in Christian ministry has increased slightly in recent decades however; there was a disparity among women in leadership in non-profit organizations compared to men (GuideStar, 2011). Women have been underrepresented in leadership within nonprofit organizations for many decades (Rivkin et al., 2014). Continuing perceptions of these roles as male specific positions have imposed considerable restraints on female Christian ministry leaders. This was primarily due to cultural perceptions, cultural behaviors, and cultural diversity (Paustian-Underdahl et al., 2014).

Cultural styles form the perception of what was considered a good leader, especially in making decisions. The perception of a leader was the understanding of what is right, wrong, fair, and morally correct, which has nothing to do with gender. A female Christian ministry leader has the ability to meet the guidelines when decisions are made according to the overall benefit of serving in Christian ministry and eliminates the need to benefit self. When society removes biases, prejudices, and discriminations, people are able to view leadership from a broader prospective and adapt to a global mindset without defense or offense (Bacha & Walker, 2013). The leader's ability to exert power, influence, and authority effectively depends upon the understanding of cultural differences and the ability to gain the respect level of other leaders and the followers.

Some cultures relate power to dominance or being able to dictate to an individual or group without explanation or collaboration (Ott, 2011). In other cultures, power represents the ability to mobilize and activate people, things, and groups without force or coercion. Similar to power, authority was perceived in various cultures as only one individual having the control to determine what was right or wrong and any other contribution that was acceptable (Marsh, 2013). However, there are cultures that view authority as the ability to receive consultation from a leader that was deemed as a respected expert and the expert opinion of the leader weighs heavier in decision making. Just as power and authority dictate the different perceptions of what was ethical, leadership influence has a great effect as well. Influence in many cultures signifies respect earned by a leader through motivation, inspiration, and the ability of the leader to make an impact (Vevere, 2014). Leaders with great influence are appreciated for guidance, direction, and instruction, which are viewed similar in most cultures. Leaders without influence experience less production, effort, and vitality within an organization. Culture shapes an organization through leadership, but leadership must have power, influence, and authority in order to see productive results.

Appropriate perceptions include learning the value of diversity and avoiding biases, stereotypes, unfairness, discrimination, and inappropriate behaviors. It was important that leaders and recipients of diverse cultures have a level of competence regarding personal culture values and worldviews. A valuable method to include to cultural perceptions, cultural behaviors, and cultural diversity was flexibility (Sawyer, 2016). Flexibility and respect regarding the different views required the most important communication tool, which was listening. The leader and team must be respectful in listening to other beliefs and cultural views that are present (Gupta, 2011). Respect and listening to others assisted in influencing the behaviors of individuals and the team. Individuals feel that there was no opportunity to be heard, it causes a sense of hostility and reluctance. The leader and the team need to be able to have a voice and to be heard.

Leadership within itself is sacrificial and requires much discipline. Although leaders are still learning, the greatest attribute was being able to relate to others in a positive way. As a leader, the position provides opportunity to encounter many different people and several cultural perceptions. Those perceptions can be found challenging to some leaders, but it encourages leaders to operate in an ethical manner that serves others with respect, honesty, equality, and justice. The behaviors of leaders are what followers see and imitate as an example. It is imperative that leaders treat others with dignity, serve others in humility, ensure fairness, and provide honesty. Leaders have the responsibility and ability to shape an organizations culture for the better.

Theoretical Foundation

Theoretical framework was defined as a pair of theoretical assumptions that define the relationship among a set of phenomena. Therefore, a theoretical framework can be described as an interrelationship among constructions, definitions, and propositions of a present condition within a usual phenomenon. The theoretical framework examined the theories relating to understanding female Christian ministry leaders.

This research study utilized theories and findings from several sources to help better understand the phenomenon of female Christian ministry leaders and the experiences that drive the phenomenon. This section of the chapter discussed the following theories that provided a clear view to the study: (a) Servant Leadership and (b) Inclusive Leadership. Each theory is relevant to how perceptions and barriers relate to women desiring to serve in leadership, while addressing the significance of including male and female without bias, discrimination, or prejudice. These theories helped the researcher in data collection, data analysis, and interpretation. The foundation of this study was Servant leadership theory and Inclusive leadership theory both provided a base for understanding this phenomenon. Servant leadership, according to Greenleaf (1977) is a natural desire to sacrifice by people for people. Servant leadership includes male and female leaders with an innate feeling stirring one to lead as a service rather than be lead. Inclusive leadership provides a confirms the prospective of Servant leadership that includes a diverse population with different perceptions, but with the need to find commonalities to enhance the well-being of individuals, groups, and organizations (Jaworski, 2012)

The different leadership theories that are effective in Christian ministry can be interchangeable and in some instances, many of the elements can be combined. Christian ministry encompasses the desire to teach and serve by expressing the heart of God through meeting the needs of others. The goal is for the leader to make the greatest impact possible in the lives of followers while also maturing in the journey. The aspects of servant leadership and inclusive leadership nurtured, develop, and culture both the leader and followers in Christian ministry. Although, Christian ministry usually implements one theory or another, it could be helpful to take intricate elements from each theory to gain even better results.

Greenleaf's 1977, Servant Leadership theory proposed a model based primarily on helping others to grow as individuals and within the community (Kemp, 2016). Servant leadership was important to this study because serving others is not gender specific and provides a foundational standard for female Christian ministry leader to serve regardless of gender barriers (Berger, 2014). Servant leadership was relevant to this study because it identified the need and importance for leaders to serve selfless with great sacrifice. Servant leadership expresses the requirement for not only service but also most importantly sacrifices. Sacrifice is having the ability to press beyond hindrances and barriers that are internally and externally present. Servant leadership theory was useful to the study because it transcends perceptions of people and it was not limited to society or tradition. The researcher examined the personal, social, and perceptual barriers that female Christian ministry leaders face in Christian ministry. It also identified the inherent and learned characteristics necessary for Christian leadership. Servant leadership theory provided a base for understanding this phenomenon. Servant leadership is a theory that demonstrates and has characteristics of serving others, which is a major factor in leadership. Servant leadership is geared toward serving more than leadership, even if you are a leader. Servant leadership is about being an example and role model or mentor to others, sacrifice on the behalf of others, meeting the needs of others and providing direction, guidance and training to develop one another in humility (Jenkins, 2014). Servant leadership is training both the leader and developing the followers, so that the leaders and followers continue to grow.

Servant leadership is a foundational theory that involves everyone (Koshal, 2005). Servant Leadership demonstrates unity of all including age, gender, nationalities, and cultures. As the world and society changes, Servant leadership is the foundation that makes adaptability and change flow smoothly. Servant leadership is a non-traditional theory designed for an individual and organization to develop, grow, and extend outwardly to others. It encompasses continued growth and discipline for not just the followers from the leader, but for both to be balanced (Doh & Quigley, 2014). The servant has an expected responsibility servicing the needs of all, without hesitation, biases, discrimination, or preferences. (Doh & Quigley, 2014). Leadership that is accountable and trustworthy exceeds cultural preferences, traditions, and barriers to inspire. Servant leadership motivates, cultivate standards, approaches, and actions for individuals and groups and the organization as a whole. (Greenleaf, 1977).

Additionally, Inclusive leadership provided a prospective that included diverse perceptions, but with the need to find and understand relatable common places to enhance the well-being of individuals, groups, and organizations (Jaworski, 2012). Inclusive leadership logically fits into this research study because it includes everyone as in a sense of community demonstrated that everyone is needed. Every selfless contribution of service of a leader can have a great impact and influence on others. Inclusive leadership is important to female Christian ministry leaders because there is a need to find a common place and remove barriers (Tidball, 2012). Inclusive leadership comprehends the need for diverse cultures and promotes ways to increase acceptance while broadening perspectives. Inclusive leadership distributes power and mutual respect so that one group or individual is not in total control (Beaty & Davis, 2012). Inclusive leadership places human relationships as priority, which is an element that gives definition to an organization. Inclusive leadership encompasses more than the financial and operational things of an organization, but it values human relationship and people. For female leadership positions, the inclusive leadership model provides a way to consider leaders without bias. A trait of inclusive leadership is respect for individuals and groups while removing self-initiatives and self-implementation through power, which works well when considering women who are seeking advancement in non-profit organizations. An inclusive leadership trait understands the importance and value of people with a genuine concern. An inclusive leader is in support of diversity and develops patterns to develop such behaviors that fostered unity and teamwork. Inclusive leadership promotes creativity and commitment to serving. Resourcefulness is a characteristic of all leaders and the absence of discrimination towards female Christian ministry leaders and gender preferences creativity enhances nonprofit organizations (Suk Bong, Thi Bich Hanh, & Byung, 2015). Inclusive leadership aids servant leadership as a foundation to support women serving in Christian ministry.

A trait of inclusive leadership is selflessness and placing the priorities of other before selfish ambitions. Inclusive leaders purposely reach out and extend a level of openness to make everyone feel comfortable. Included in the inclusive leadership traits is the leader being intentional about developing, promoting, and recruiting individuals that exhibited relatable traits that are accepting to diversity. Nevertheless, if an individual or group is not familiar with being in a diverse group, the inclusive leader works to develop such behaviors to increase the momentum of the organization. An inclusive leader promotes and develops individuals through sharing experiences and providing a level of transparency so that others can easily relate. Inclusive leadership includes the leader creating an environment of mutual respect and being a living example of integrity. An inclusive leader, leads by influence and not aggressive authority.

Because there are some women that have been successful in serving as a leader in Christian ministry despite barriers, the study examined what measures women have taken to overcome social, cultural, and perceptual barriers, which educated future generations of women seeking leadership in Christian ministry (Michailidis et al., 2012). The research questions will identify inherent and learned characteristics that are evident due to perceived expectations of society and culture for women seeking leadership positions (Wienclaw, 2015)

While there was ample literature that explored female Christian ministry leaders, this study examined an area that has been under represented in literature, i.e., how women perceive the constraints and their own leadership abilities. (Johns, 2013). Exploring the perceptions and experiences of female Christian ministry leader's abilities has developed strategies to overcome barriers and attain success. The research of this study extended both theories, because it provided a strategy or strategies that helped female leaders to overcome barriers and be successful in Christian ministry.

Review of the Literature

The review of literature consisted of a substantial amount of books, research papers, and publications to identify barriers are present for female Christian ministry leaders in nonprofit organizations. Although there is a consistent expansion on leadership, the literature does not provide any empirical studies on the self-perceptions of the experiences of women in leadership for nonprofit organizations. The review of literature initially revealed the personal, social, and perceptual barriers that women face when they seek leadership in Christian ministry (Scott,

2010). Secondly, the review of the literature revealed the measures that women have taken to overcome these barriers (Michailidis et al., 2012). Thirdly, the literature revealed the inherent and learned characteristics that are necessary for Christian leadership (Wienclaw, 2015).

Society and culture have taught women to become operative leaders by incapacitating these barriers. The female Christian ministry leaders' experiences exposed obstacles as well as defined approaches for success in Christian ministry. By analyzing the experiences of women in leadership position, the researcher recognized and classified the perception of their experiences. The phenomenon is how women in leadership perceive their experiences in Christian ministry. Some female Christian ministry leaders have overcome barriers. Female Christian ministry leaders are subject to the veracity of biases, favoritism, and discrimination. These barriers are largely present due to cultural perceptions and actions. Women in leadership cope with internal and external barriers in

Christian ministry. The examination of their experiences identified bridges to improve societal perceptions. The purpose of this qualitative case study was to explore how women perceived and overcame social, cultural, and perceptual barriers to succeed as leaders in Christian ministry (Scott, 2010). Secondly, to examine what methods women have taken to overcome these barriers (Michailidis et al., 2012). Thirdly, to identify inherent and learned characteristics that is essential for Christian leadership (Wienclaw, 2015)

Gaining an understanding of how women in Christian leadership identify and perceive internal and external barriers accomplished the purpose of this study, which is to discover barriers, steps taken to overcome barriers, and why women endure despite obstacles. The "how" question identifies the current problem, which is that the observations of internal and external barriers regarding this phenomenon continue to be unknown. Discovering the "what" question provided information unknown regarding the achievement of some women. Answering the posed "why" question investigated deeper into the phenomenon by expanding upon perseverance of women to overcome barriers, furthering the study, and better addressed the purpose and problem of this study. The qualitative methodology with a qualitative case study design makes answering these questions possible by allowing participants to describe, in detail, their perceptions, accounts, and experiences with the phenomenon (Yin, 2009).

Leadership is not loud, boisterous, and driven by being seen or in control of others. It is however, being disciplined and secure in life so that others can see an example of what is expected. Leaders stand as an example willing to abide by standards, principles, and a process of submitting their own lives, regardless of gender. Likewise, the leader is not swayed or persuaded by the opinions of others but rather listen attentively to the recommendations that are offered as a training tool. Additionally, the leader keeps in mind that change is necessary and uses influence to help in the process. It is not a title or a position that makes a leader. The leader gives definition and meaning to the title. Actually, an authentic, true, born, leader is not in need of a title. A leader is something that you choose through service. Leadership is a service to the world and serves a greater purpose in life. Expectations are of a person in leadership regardless of gender.

Servant as a leader is demonstrated and has characteristics of serving others, which is a major factor in leadership (Doh & Quigley, 2014). Leadership is geared toward serving more than leadership, even if you are a leader. Leadership is being an example and mentor to others when needed, while cultivating others through proper direction, lawful guidance and in depth training to develop one another in humility (Jenkins, 2014). Leadership is training both the leader and developing the followers, so that the leaders and followers continued to grow. Leadership is a foundational theory that involves everyone (Koshal, 2005). Female Christian ministry leaders have the same responsibilities regarding leadership; however, cultural barriers are constantly present as hurdles for women to jump over in order to serve.

Being a servant leader positions the leader as seeking to know and understand other's concerns, thoughts, and ideas without ignoring other's concepts and ideas. The individual and personal thoughts of a leader do not supersede the needs of others. Servant Leadership is a non-traditional theory designed for an individual and organization to develop, grow, and extend outwardly to others. It encompasses continued growth and discipline for not just the followers from the leader, but for both to be balanced. One main concept is in order to understand leadership; you must also understand being a follower. Additionally, collaboration amongst the leader and followers enables support from the leader to the follower and from the follower to the leader. Both participants become encouraged and enablers of one another to reach their ultimate potential. The overall characteristics of Servant Leadership are that leaders are not selfish but selfless (Greenleaf, 1977).

The common elements of effective leadership are serving others, establishing relationships, and influence (Doh & Quigley, 2014). Leadership is assessed by the effectiveness of service to render to others without forsaking oneself. Effective leadership understands the value of relationship and one of the greatest assets of leadership is to be able to relate to others, and the influence leadership should have on followers (Rivkin et al., 2014). The servant leadership theory is all inclusive of giving service to everyone regardless of status, position, intellect. The service element includes serving others with fairness, standards, and principles that eliminates prejudice, biases, and discrimination (Chen, Zhu, & Zhou, 2014). Leader attends graciously and willingly to the needs of the organization and the people. Effective leaders adhere to rules, regulations, guidelines, and general practices that encourage others to do so as well. As a leader that meets the needs of others, it is done with great sacrifice and a willingness to see others transform.

Effect leadership is assessed with the vision, mission, and goals being evidently displayed within the organization. Likewise, the foundation of leadership is to give sacrificially through knowledge, understanding, and transparency (Chen et al., 2014). Sharing life experiences and encounters helped in eliminating disappointments, which helped others not to make the same mistakes. Leaders have the awesome task of making certain that others have a better understanding. Having the right information to apply to the right situation can transform a life experience into a positive encounter (Koshal, 2005). It is the perception of experiences that can ignite culture barriers for female Christian ministry leaders. It is hard to be effective with barriers that exist because of culture and self-perceptions.

Historically, gender has played a pivotal role in whether or not women should receive Christian Ministry Leadership positions. The societal perception of women has been passed down through cultural teachings while misrepresenting female Christian ministry leaders (Vasavada, 2012). Women in leadership have not always been accepted due to tradition and cultural perceptions, regardless women should not eliminate their leadership assignments. (Bacha & Walker, 2013). Daily presentations unveil with many different cultural values that encompass the way people think and act. Although the intent is to have a personal belief system that does not necessarily affect others, the reality is beliefs turn into patterns of behavior. It is the perceptions and behavior patterns within various cultures that shape the worldview. Even cultures that are consistent with isolating other individuals and groups still have an influence on others including the Christian ministry (Meyer, 2010). Since, individuals and groups make up an organization, it is essential to implement a strategy that engaged all cultures. Reviewing the influence that culture has in Christian ministry, barriers and self-perceptions are evidence that there are opposing roles to its existence (Rogers, 2010).

Barriers and self-perceptions have the ability to cause deformity, however as Christian ministry engages in a strategy of love, unity, and trust, false perception overrode (Hong, 2012). Cultural barriers produce an attitude and behavior that people exhibit in a culture where self is priority by choice (Stob, 1968). It poses as a challenge, especially in the United States for individuals and groups to understand other viewpoints. Cultural barriers are not an advocate of group integration, bonding, or connecting to anything that stood in the way of personal advancement. Cultural barriers are in effect when we neglect the needs of society as a whole and deem one group's perception as more important. It is making decisions and taking actions without giving any regard to what others may think, encounter, or experience because of it (Stob, 1968).

Social (non-business) interaction is a key element in an organization. It can be used as a learning tool that enhances understanding between diverse groups while teaching ways that helped them relate to one another. This would also include the relationship from leader to follower. Non-business interaction could be a way of breaking the ice and extending an open door for those that were not quite sure of how to interact with leadership. The significance of social non-business interaction is to remove the tension and allow individuals and groups within the organization to be comfortable. Social non-business interaction can identify what stimulates individuals or groups to produce at full capacity. When people are not open and comfortable with sharing, collaborating, or being in a team, they tend to hold back. Social non-business interaction provides time for diverse people, with diverse cultures to interact with one another. There are some instances where problems can arise, however, problems arise every day and part of understanding one another is learning how to relate to each other even when problems exist. An apprehension the organization could possibly have is confusion present the workplace from a non-business social event.

Cultural preferences most significantly influence the social interaction style of an organization, because of what is traditionally accepted within each diverse culture. However, if an organization can find a way to include all of the cultural differences as a supportive learning tool, then the highlight can be placed on the similarities. Similarities will allow commonalities to outweigh the differences. Although cultures can be different, people can still find a way to identify with one another.

Christian ministry leaders meet challenges in adhering to a code of ethics that often is not understood, interpreted, or accepted by other Christian ministry leaders which stimulates division (Ştefan, 2008). Division attacks unity and promotes confusion, which alters perception and interpretation globally (Ryan et al., 2011). However, what is the greater concern is Christian ministry leaders expressing a togetherness of shared values and eliminating individual perceptions (Kessler, 2013). A global code of ethics is capable of providing direction, guidance, and discipline (Romani & Szkudlarek, 2014). The elements within the global code of ethics are a mirrored example of the Bible. Interpretation, acceptance, agreement, unity, and implementation unified the personal and professional ethics of Christian ministry leaders (Bacha & Walker, 2013). Christian ministry leaders are to impact lives, but the life of the Christian ministry leader must also receive a God impact that transcends globally (Valk, 2010).

A common code of ethics to Christian ministry leaders globally is feasible and can be created and disseminated with accountability in a general and detail format (Ryan et al., 2011). The dissemination process would come through the word of God outlined in the Bible, which is also the foundation for formulating a global code of ethics for Christian ministry leaders. The structure to disseminate a common code of ethics for Christian ministry leadership globally would be through relationship. Relationship is in the levels of personal individual relationships with God (Marshall, 2008). Through sustaining and maintaining a relationship with God, which is the basis for Christian leadership, connections are developed and appreciated.

Additionally, the disseminating method would also be through unity. Unity of Christian leaders being seen, heard, and experienced through various diverse communities globally (Valk, 2010). Every leader should demonstrate the code of ethics within each culture, environment, and atmosphere. Relationship and unity does not mean that it is possible for every Christian leader to come together physically or in the natural, but it is mostly addressing the ability to come into agreement of the code of ethics, apply it daily, and disseminate it globally through examples. Relationships and unity provide a cohesive position, prospective, and posture amongst Christian leadership (Ryan et al., 2011). The dissemination of a global code of ethics was a great sacrifice for Christian leaders to participate in while gaining a mutual understanding, concept, and perspective to grasp the dissemination efforts. The dissemination process, if not carefully done, by Christian leaders were overshadowed by government. Government can implement a global code of ethics that Christian ministry leaders should follow and regardless of individual perceptions, it would still have to be followed.

Leaders really should be interested in the ethical management of an organization because it is the driving force behind what decisions are made and how the decisions are carried out. Ethics give some form of guidance and structure that allowed the organization to accomplish what is necessary and viable for every participant. Leaders have many things to lose when an organization is managed unethical. Leaders may lose people, respect, and influence, all due to unethical behaviors (Donaldson, 1996). Likewise, it is not the dividends or the size of the organization that matters. It is the quality of services that are being provided along with the connections and relationships that are being built through individuals, leaders, and community (Chau,

2011). It is also important that we establish an ethical relationship with other companies and organizations that we are working with. It does not matter the size or the dividends if at the end of the day there is always a risk of losing everything because of a bad decision. At some point, all organizations should maintain a level of ethical stability. Organizations must also show the stakeholders a level of honesty, trustworthiness, and commitment. The overall goal is to grow appropriately and properly. Advancing too fast or experiencing a decline quickly is never good, but a good steady flow is always necessary within an organization.

Ethical governance gives some guarantee to the organizations viability because it shows what the organization is capable of and the capacity or maturity the organization has to implement what is necessary. Viability indicates that an organization is able to sustain and express a reasonable amount of success. Being a well-balanced organization that is practical and that is taking practical steps to remain in a certain position. There are organizations that are closing down for the mere fact that they are not being practical and applying ethical governance (Donaldson, 1996). Every organization has to be cognizant of the energy, environment, and atmosphere that promote ethical behavior. Ethics starts at the top and flows down to give an all-around ethical effect (Chau, 2011). Sometimes it may take changing some things but it is worth it and it is something that must be done in order to be able to give a guarantee. It cannot be a seasonal or periodic episode but it must be constant for every participant of the organization. The only true way to guarantee organization's viability is to adhere to the guidelines set forth and when error is made, it is quickly corrected.

Women in various leadership positions have learned to adapt and adopt many of the cultural perceptions. Their behaviors have also challenged the set traditions and rituals by going beyond the norm through reaching for what they are purposed to do (Paustian-Underdahl et al., 2014). Cultural barriers have become a training tool for women in leadership to gain knowledge and influence in Christian ministry (Vevere, 2014). Cultural behaviors of women are a learned or adopted attitude that enables uncertain behaviors that are relative to pleasing the traditions of culture. Each culture has its own individualistic concept regarding female Christian ministry leaders and it does not contribute to benefit the nonprofit organization. A more in-depth concept is that cultural behaviors are not just specific to an individual person, but it includes groups with particular perspective regarding female Christian ministry leaders. Cultural behaviors are concepts used to make decisions that cause a certain behavior without consulting other groups for understanding (Rogers, 2010). The concept capitalizes on endorsing the quality and lifestyle of self, which opposes concerted opinions.

The servant leadership model has expectations of the leader being responsible for servicing the needs of all, rather than attending to the individual biases due to favoritism. Servant leadership expects the leader to maintain an intimate relationship with God that enables the leader to give guidance and direction that benefited all. Servant leadership transcends beyond cultural preferences, traditions, and boundaries to inspire. Servant leadership motivates, nurtures values, attitudes, and behaviors for the leader and the followers. Additionally, servant leadership keeps leaders in a position that is unique and balanced. As a leader, implementing the servant leadership theory is justifiable by promoting teamwork. Teamwork, which consists of leaders, followers, and stakeholders, made everyone interested in a positive productive outcome. Servant leadership expresses the position of the leader as a servant first to others, then to God, and sacrificing self totally. Servant leadership holds the leader as a servant, but not as someone that is on a pedestal and untouchable. Relationships are established between leaders and followers through service. As leaders serve, lessons are learned through being able to relate to one another. Servant leadership articulates the leadership position to be competent with the ability to influence through self-behavior, attitude, and personal values that influenced others through hope, faith, and love.

Female Christian ministry leaders are influencing the nature of diversity and women in leadership are fostering relationships between diversity, Christian ministry, and society Virick & Greer (2012). Gender differences within certain organizations are classified by a variety of metaphors, that signify biases and discriminatory barriers that hinder women in leadership (Smith et al., 2012). Cook (2010) addresses the hidden discriminatory acts that demonstrate the rejection of diversity. Dzubinski, (2012) regards many women leaders as lost because of not being included in leadership and Christian ministry. The perception is, leaders must have a vision, and women are not visionaries. If a woman represents qualities of leadership, some cultures perceive it as a violation. The stereotype leads to a belief that women leaders are not needed or respected. Similar to Dzubinski (2012) and Bush (2012), Cook (2010), agrees with the negative perception that has penetrated the minds of people regarding female Christian ministry leaders. Bush (2012) differently uses the term multicultural, which pertains to the diversity of cultures to include gender, race, and culture. However, similar to Dzubinski (2012), culture is major element of diversity and distinguishes what is acceptable. Dzubinski (2012) identified the culture, environment, and nature within the expectations of leadership.

Dzubinski (2012) found that many women leaders are lost because of the lack of inclusion within ministry and mission efforts. However, requests their insight as it is a great influence. The perception is that women are second-class citizens, which reduces participation. Additionally, the perception is, leaders must have a vision, and women are not visionaries. If a woman possesses qualities of leadership, the community perceives it as a violation. The stereotype shows that women in leadership are not respected. Similar to Dzubinski (2012) and Bush (2012), Cook (2010) findings agree with the negative perception that has penetrated the minds of people regarding women in leadership. Bush (2012) differently uses the term multicultural, which pertains to the diversity of cultures to include gender, race, and culture. However, similar to Dzubinski (2012), culture is major element of diversity and distinguishes what is acceptable. Dzubinski (2012) identified the culture, environment, and nature within the expectations of leadership. Cook (2010) addresses the hidden discriminatory acts that demonstrate the rejection of diversity. Many opportunities exist in teaching, evangelizing, preaching, and singing but only a selected few with approval for the task and diversity is present but limited the category of gender.

Dzubinski (2012) used a sample of women in leadership that live in China and Samaria, and compared the theological views and issues of women spreading the gospel. Differently, Bush (2012) uses the experiences of Baptist pastors as a model to define multicultural and diverse actions within ministry. The method used was to examine the women that are mission oriented and often do ministry in nations that devalue women, which is quite similar to Cook (2010). An appreciated approach is how Dzubinski (2012) inserted practical steps toward change for women in leadership. Bush (2012) takes note of God's plan and purpose for every individual life and women in leadership is not just an option but is a normal trend. Christ died for us all and every gender, race, culture, and person was included. Diversity is unity within Christ's community (Bush, 2012). Christian ministry is a place of freedom and liberty, which undergird diversity. However, there is a great percentage of women oppressed by a leader perceived as the oppressor in ministry that the oppressor (Cook, 2010).

Virick & Greer (2012) suggests that diversity in leadership is critical to the success of any organization. The development of women leaders is through education and mentorship is a favorable step to balancing diversity in an organization. With a survey study of top managers and executives, it indicates that females positively affect the performance, climate, and relationships within an organization. The study found that women are going beyond the boundaries that are evident (Ragins, Townsend, & Mattis, 1998). Ruiz-Jimenez & Fuentes-Fuentes (2016) hypothesized the reduction of negative effects with gender diversity within teams. Many effects are captivated because team participants have the tendency to relate according to similarities. However, in order for a team to be effective, the differences of each individual have positive outcomes. To appreciate the differences every participant must be supportive of one another rather than just cooperative of each other. Yancey (1999) explored that the acceptance of racial diversity usually includes the equality of gender diversity. The research study examined the liberation of attitudes regarding race, which is the leading stimulant to gender diversity in Christian ministry. The data information for the study was retrieved by mail with a survey sent to several churches within a metropolitan area with multicultural environments. Out of 904 churches 488 responded to the survey.

Theology of leadership is a consensual, sacrificial, imparted, and imputed covenant agreement between a leader and God (Mark 10:45). Theology of leadership consists of a personal and communal integration that encapsulates the ability for the leader to continually develop (1 Peter 5:2). The leader should be able to influence with his/her behavior, attitude, choices, experiences, and lifestyle (2 Timothy 2:15). Through the intimate and personal relationship with God, the leader is able to give guidance and direction with confidence and with the ability to translate God's word through applicable messages and teachings. Likewise, the leader should demonstrate a vision, mission, and goal that is specifically designed and tasked for him/her and the people who are following him/her (Acts 2:28). The leader should also be authentic in application, supplication, and presentation as he/she leads people along a given journey (Numbers 27:17).

Theology of leadership is a systematic and biblical concept; however, it should not be a limited aspect that stifles the leader or the people. A systematic formation should be followed to maintain order and respect. Nevertheless, most importantly, there should always be a biblical aspect that gives the foundation for theology of leadership. The systematic formation includes standards and principles that are set by God to benefit those that follow biblical direction. The biblical aspect includes the detail experiences of leaders that dealt with many of the same issues, challenges, and situations as those of every generation (Proverbs 29:2). The ultimate goal is for the leader and follower to know God through relationship while being elevated through spiritual development.

The most important component of the definition is the personal relationship a leader has with God. Just as he/she leads, they too must also be subject to a leader. This is significant in my ministry because it allows me as a leader to be accountable, responsible, but also to be corrected. A leader is still learning, developing, and in need of guidance. Additionally, it allows growth to take place and leaders to be continually elevated as well, it allowed the followers also to be increased, multiplied, and stretched. It removes complacency and adds strength, substance, and support.

The most significant challenge of engaging the community through service and leadership is meeting the needs both physically and spiritually with balance. Within a community, there are different cultures, beliefs, and religions that are merged together that do not always agree. The challenge is to respond appropriately without showing biases or offending others. Although, there may not be the initial agreement of topics, issues, and situations, the practical challenge is to endure through understanding and love (Bosch, 1993). In addition to endurance and understanding, it is crucial that leaders of society treat others fairly, regardless of whether the involved parties agree or not. Often times leaders are challenged with showing favor toward those that are in our culture, group, or belief while disregarding others because it is out of our comfort zone.

Leaders must accept the challenge to stick to the overall mission of the Christian ministry, which is to meet the needs of others and close the gap. We must be relevant, relatable, and real by abiding in love. Love gives us the ability to handle every situation correctly, confront issues that have the ability to diminish relationships, and come together to pursue a common purpose. Leaders have to adapt to the things of the world but not adopt the things of the world. We adapt to function in a world that is full of different perspectives that engage many different behaviors. However, through understanding, tolerance, and love, those behaviors can be transformed. Tolerance is having patience with other beliefs and not humanly being an opposition, but spiritually abiding in truth and love (Carson, 2012). It is a leader's job to service within the community, to be active in doing good works, and to be an example through relationship and servant hood.

Leadership Theory Research plays a vital role in structuring and applying the personal theology of leadership by being the foundation to posture servant hood, practical teaching, balanced living, and relational transformation. Having a posture of servant hood provides the key element for formulating a structure that will last with the ability to grow, enlarge, increase, and expand. Practical teaching is a component that provides details of the servant hood structure through relevant and transparent stories that can be understood by followers and other leaders. It is through growth and development that lives begin to transform. Leadership Theory Research is the key to maintaining a current outlet to reach others for what is taking place in the world now. Leadership Theory Research changed constantly with inspiration, guidance, and direction from God. There is no one set theory that can reach everyone, at different times, a new concept created specifically, and particularly for any situations that may arise. Through relationship, the leader can serve God, mentor other leaders, and serve in the community to meet the needs of the people. Leadership theory role is to serve as a foundation that transformed the lives of the leader, followers, mentors, individuals, and groups.

Leadership theory influences the mentorship style of a leader by what perceptions and perspectives of biblical interpretation and leadership theory has been adopted. Leaders train, develop, and mentor others according to what theories and biblical teachings they have received in the past, whether it is right or wrong. Likewise, there is a great influence on the mentorship style of a leader if he/she has not taken into consideration the current times in which people are living. Proper perception and interpretation of experiences is critical to knowing what leadership theory works best for the environment, situations, and circumstances that people face today, especially for Christian Ministry Leadership, because it is a service to people (Chung, 2011). What leaders and mentors used to encounter are very different from what is being encountered now. Many of the struggles and life challenges are very different from times past and much more intense. Leadership theory that is properly interpreted to become applicable for present times had great influence on the mentorship style of leadership. Therefore, it helped those that are being mentored to understand how to be relevant for today, which may be considered some radical changes (Kohl, 2006). Leaders without relevance in regards to cultural behaviors, cultural diversity, and cultural perceptions will not know how to relate, through leadership theory and can damage the influence of the mentor's style of leadership.

There is an even greater influence when the leader is able to do group mentorship that includes the female Christian ministry leader and those that are seeking leadership positions in Christian ministry. Mentorship is about relationship, but mentoring on an individual basis within a group is like having the best of both worlds (Vogel & Finkelstein, 2011). In a group, each individual experienced things that are normally not included in an individual setting. Group settings inspire, motivate, enlighten, encourage, and strengthen. Each participant can learn valuable lessons from one another as well as learning to grow together as a team, which is definitely a great influence to have. Teamwork and unity provides access for everyone to see different perspectives and experience the mentor being able to relate to everyone in a group setting which truly gives a picture of what is expected of a leader. It takes time for leaders to meet individually, but it can be a more productive meeting in a group setting to teach the same lesson or provide the demonstration that is needed. Additionally, as questions, recommendations, and suggestions are made, everyone will receive additional insight that enriched and edify. Group mentorship requires a level of discipline and maturity that removes selfishness along with sacrifice. Therefore included in a group are the differences regarding gender roles and the discussion of various experiences that enlightened another group (Kaufmann, Harrel, Milam, Woolverton, & Miller, 1986). You can have several groups within a crowd and that makes group mentoring very interesting.

Andronoviene (2013) argues that women have the qualities necessary for leadership. With training, development, and coaching, women recently are experiencing the respect and encouragement deserved as a leader. Additionally, women have the ability to achieve standards but also lead vigorously presenting excellence as a standard. Women lead with more passion and fervency with the tools provided such as education, mentorship and coaching (Andronoviene, 2013). Newkirk and Cooper (2013) differently discussed that mentorship is not adequate, but an individual in leadership should receive a formal theological education. England (2011) is in agreement with Andronoviene (2013) and Newkirk & Cooper (2013) concerning the importance of mentorship. However, Newkirk & Cooper (2013) and England (2011) similarly to Andronoviene (2013) communicated that mentorship and internships are necessary for preparing women in leadership. Similar to Andronoviene (2013), Newkirk & Cooper (2013) use a professional analogy of a medical student that trains and receives a degree, so must women in leadership.

The subject of qualification, standards, and passion of women in leadership provided by Andronoviene (2013) gives a significant and substantial view of the need for women in leadership. Newkirk & Cooper (2013) expressed the importance of effective leadership particularly women in ministry as being just equally important as the careers as those in the medical profession. England (2011) discussed the order or headship within the Bible and the areas for women to assist in the church, but indicates the need for women leaders in the church. The methods, within the research, are sturdy and provide definition. Andronoviene (2013) described practice as an activity that an individual is willing to participate whether complex or simple. During the process, the individual realized the need for a standard or excellence. Newkirk & Cooper (2013) also expressed the difficulty faced by women in leadership, but mentors can help women operate in success. Andronoviene (2013) mentioned finding creative ways of leadership for women and although that is an idea to ponder, the gap remains of the quality in the path that women take to leadership. Newkirk & Cooper (2013) and England (2011) have gaps that do not provide suggestions for women beyond the perceptions and limits.

England (2011) used a sample of Pentecostal women, which is specific to a particular denomination, and not necessarily the requirements of women in other denominations. Newkirk & Cooper (2013) has a sample of African American Women within the Baptist Church. Andronoviene (2013) has a sample that is general to women in leadership and does not specify a particular denomination.

Haddad (2013a) addresses the need for women in leadership to be confident and possess skills and abilities to have balance with ministry and family. Leadership alone is very demanding, selfless, and sacrificial (Arvey, Zhang, Avolio, & Krueger, 2007). Women in leadership must have faith and courage, which comes through daily devotion and biblical study. Relationships between leaders and individuals within the church have the ability to produce healthy relationships if the underlying issues of women in leadership are visible. Training, development, and mentorship empowered women and instill confidence (Haddad, 2013b).

Mock (2005) suggests that there are boundaries set forth in many religious institutions because of the conforming to religious traditions. As the constant argument continues over the role of women in the church, a barrier still exists even within Christian Education for women. An individual's life is stifled because of the different interpretations of what is acceptable. The method used in this study was a qualitative case study that explored women leaders within Seminary. The sample was with women administrators employed in Christian Education.

Thomas (2014) supports the use of a strategic training plan for equipping women for leadership. Thomas (2014) found it effective that one of the details of the plan is to use matured females that have the experience necessary to develop another young woman with less experience. Training and development consist of hands on weekly applications with biblical implications and church situations. The sample project was with mature Christian women from inner city churches. The method that used was data retrieved from several church that included surveys and questionnaires to graduate students from Seminary. According to Mento (2014), women in leadership nurture growth, a valuable asset to Christian leadership.

Formational worship influences a Christian leader's preference in leadership theory by how effective the leader was and is. As a Christian leader, the individual disciplines, and practices that are routinely done has the greatest influence on a Christian leader's preference. It is during the disciplined rituals of meditation, evaluation, prayer, journaling, and cultivation that leaders can clearly discern the direction of God and position themselves to follow those directions (Crowley, 2014). Formational worship is the time that Christian leaders are built, restored, and their capacity increases to meet the needs of others (Noland, 2009). It is impossible to provide needed support to others when the leader themselves are not in a place to do so. Without the influence of formational worship, Christian leaders can be lacking or become deficient and will not have the ability to carry out the plans of God. Formational worship also influences the desire of the leader to want more and to do more for God and for Gods people (Scott, 2010). It is an intimate time that God pours into the Christian leader through training, development, enlightenment, and inspiration to do what is required of them. Formational worship removes the want to be selfish or have self-absorbed feelings that result into self-willed actions. Likewise, formational worship influences Christian leaders so that Christian leaders can have a positive influence on others. What is done in the private times of formational worship can then be productive in corporate time.

It is challenging to integrate leaders within a multinational organization. The challenges to integrate leaders regardless of where they come from or where they will go in reference to location were great because of individual perceptions (Northouse, 2007). Different cultures have their own definitions of power, authority, and influence. Likewise, they contribute their individual perceptions according to what they see and experience. In many cultures and instances, we do not respect power unless; it is a leader with certain position. Power in many cultures is equated to the title and position a leader holds, but in other cultures, power is referenced by a leader's integrity and character. Some cultures also equate power with money, economic status, social status, or educational status. People are more influenced by those who have a degree from a particular school or have a specific bloodline that carries a well-known name (Ng KY, Ang S, & Chan KY, 2008). Similar to interviewing for a job, many places are influenced in their decision by the type of degree a person has or where an individual received a degree. If it is a well-known, well-liked, prestigious college, then the perception is that one has more knowledge than others do who may have come from other schools. In addition, another example would be individual's ability to climb the latter because of who they know their family name and family background. Because of the different perspectives on leadership, position, authority, power, and influence, both Eastern and Western cultures would meet challenges during integration, but develop, learn, and grow as leaders, which is vital to the success of the organization. Integrating leaders can be productive or unproductive if the organization does not integrate properly with a structured process (Pearce & Conger, 2003).

The most difficult adjustment a new leader entering a multicultural workplace should expect to encounter is the challenge of gaining the necessary respect from all cultures to induce production without resistance (Bono & Judge, 2004). The leader encountered those challenges because each culture has a different prospective of what is expected from the leader and what the leader expected from them. Additionally, the leader had to find ways to relate to each culture in a way that promoted effective communication, mutual respect, and influence (Gabarro, 1987). The behaviors, styles, and traits that the leader should use to ease the adjustment is of openness, collaboration, and not making any sudden changes, but take careful evaluation of the environment and culture that currently exist. The leader must be approachable and a team player willing to take part in the success of the organization by understanding all cultures through building relationships (Bennis, 2007). The challenge of the leader was to keep the cultures cohesive and united, or if they are not united to find practical ways to do so without causing more tension. One way to ease the adjustment is through finding the leaders that has influence and power. The leaders with great influence should be sought after because they knew strategies that are currently in place and identify any changes that are needed (Bennis & Nanus, 1985). Additionally, it allows the leader to be visible with those that are respected and gain more power within the organization to influence others.

Methodology

Various research methods have been considered among researchers and the qualitative methodology was the best method for answering the research questions. Qualitative method is the total opposite of quantitative method, because it examined the barriers, experiences, and self-perceptions of distinctive individuals or specific situations within a unique perspective much like what exists for female Christian ministry leaders (Lambert & Lambert, 2012). Understanding the phenomenon was a necessity to gain justification for providing positive opportunity instead of a negative reality that can be formulated by perceptions and through experiences. Further, this study requires the qualitative methodology to gather ample data capable of providing a thick description of the phenomenon that can be effectively communicated to others (Stake, 1995). This study's phenomenon seeks richness and depth that only the qualitative methodology can provide (Stake, 1995). Moreover, the research questions rationalize the qualitative methodology.

The qualitative methodology is unlike numbers, frequencies, and amounts that are involved with quantitative research (Stake, 1995). Stake (1995) recommended a qualitative methodology design to be used as a dominant description and exploration of a phenomenon, such as the self-perceived barriers of women in Christian leadership positions. Therefore, a qualitative method was used to explore how women in leadership perceive their experiences in Christian ministry. The qualitative study provided a deeper understanding of a phenomenon through generating a deeper response to the interview questions. Qualitative researchers gather confirmation through a variety of empirical resources, such as case studies, self-analysis, personal experience, life histories, and, interviews (Yin, 2013). The case study investigated the strength of the relationship between self-identified inherent and learned characteristics of success (Stake, 1978, 1995, 1998). The qualitative methodology was the best approach for answering the research questions because it explored the barriers, experiences, and self-perceptions that existed for female Christian ministry leaders (Lambert & Lambert, 2012). Understanding this phenomenon required the qualitative methodology to dig into participants' perceptions rather than numbers, frequencies, or amounts like that of quantitative research (Singh, 2015). The qualitative case study was chosen because the mixed-methods methodology, like quantitative research, fails to focus on the perceptions of participants, thereby produced an understanding of the phenomenon (Singh, 2015). Therefore, the qualitative case study methodology was essential to understanding the posed phenomenon.

Instrumentation

This instrumentation section will report subsections on sources of data and data collection approaches. These two subsections will rationalize the use of the three sources of data and the data collection process chosen for this study. Empirical literature will be presented to justify the researcher's decision regarding data sources and the data collection process. The qualitative case study design was selected based on the need to examine the history of unique experiences and narrative self-perceptions of women in leadership. The case study research design is indispensable for this study exploring a qualitative phenomenon. Additionally, to answer the "how" research questions and explain the contemporary events over time that comprises the phenomenon, a descriptive single-case study design is selected (Yin, 2009). The common phenomenon under investigation creates a single-case study as opposed to a multiple-case study (Yin, 2009). Identifying these barriers helped to uncover hindrances to their success while serving as a leader in Christian ministry (Stake, 1995; Yin, 2009; Johnson & Christensen, 2012). The qualitative case study design was chosen so that the researcher can receive data and information from more than one primary data analysis

(Frost, 2011). Merriam (2009) explains that research focused on discovery, insight and understanding from the perspectives of those being studied offers the greatest promise of making significant contributions to the knowledge base and practice of education. Qualitative case study research approaches a problem of practice from a holistic perspective in order to gain an in-depth understanding of the situation and its meaning for those involved. The interest was in process rather than outcomes, in context rather than a specific variable, in discovery rather than in conformation. The case study research design was necessary for this study exploring a qualitative phenomenon. A case study answered the "how" and "why" research questions and explains the contemporary events over time that was the phenomenon (Yin, 2009).

Data Collection

A total sample size of 10 was appropriate to comprise a case and reach saturation (Yin, 2009). Direct involvement by the researcher using multiple sources characterized the study as qualitative. Although phenomenological research gains insightful descriptions of how an individual experiences a phenomenon (Pringle et al., 2011), case studies reflect real-life experiences and provides in-depth data from open-ended interviews making the case study most appropriate (Yin, 2009; Cronin, 2014). Case study is valuable in collecting workable data from a general population to have substantial data that is not one-sided and represents a particular group of participants that match particular characteristics or criteria (Stake, 2000). While other designs were considered, the case study design was most befitting of this research because the intent of this study was to understand Christian ministry leaders and collect a variety of data regarding experiences.

Summary

Chapter 2 began with literature review that revealed the personal, social, and perceptual barriers that women face in Christian leadership positions (Scott, 2010). Secondly, revealed what measures women have taken to overcome these barriers (Michailidis et al., 2012). Thirdly, identified were the inherent and learned characteristics crucial for Christian leadership (Wienclaw, 2015). It identified inherent and learned characteristics necessary for Christian leadership and the steps women have taken to overcome barriers. Andronoviene (2013) mentions finding creative ways of leadership for women and although that is an idea to ponder, the gap remains of the quality in the path that women take to leadership. Newkirk & Cooper (2013) and England (2011) have gaps that do not provide suggestions for women beyond the perceptions and limits. The purpose of this qualitative case study was to explore how women perceived and overcame social, cultural, and perceptual barriers to succeed as leaders in Christian ministry (Ryan et al., 2011). The internal, external, and self-perceived barriers that exist for women in Christian ministry leadership examined through direct interaction with the participants (Johnson & Christensen, 2012). The phenomenon studied was how women in leadership identify their involvements as leaders, how they explain their own learned and inherent characteristics, why they continue in this profession, and how they compete with barriers in Christian ministry within the United States.

It was not known how women perceived and overcame social, cultural, and perceptual barriers to succeed as leaders in Christian ministry. Examining female Christian ministry leaders' experiences with internal and external barriers provided a basis for understanding what these barriers are, and how to negate those barriers (Christian & Zippay, 2012). According to Mento (2014), women in leadership nurture growth, a valuable asset to Christian leadership. This study seeks to understand how women perceive their personal obstacles in Christian leadership. Further, this research will reveal the personal, social, and perceptual barriers that women face when they seek Christian leadership positions and what some have done to overcome these barriers.

This literature review will include information pertaining to cultural perception of women and how historically, gender has played a pivotal role in whether or not women receive Christian Ministry Leadership positions. The societal perception of women has been passed down through cultural teachings while misrepresenting female Christian ministry leaders (Vasavada, 2012). Women in leadership have not always been accepted due to tradition and cultural perceptions, regardless women should not eliminate their leadership assignments. (Bacha & Walker, 2013). Additionally, discussion was about the cultural behaviors of women in various leadership positions have learned to adapt and adopt many of the cultural perceptions. Their behaviors have also challenged the set traditions and rituals by going beyond the norm by reaching for what they are purposed to do (Paustian-Underdahl et al., 2014).

Inclusive of cultural perception and cultural behaviors, a continued discussion of cultural barriers examined a training tool for women in leadership to gain knowledge and influence in Christian ministry (Vevere, 2014). Gender diversity in leadership examines female Christian ministry leaders are influencing the nature of diversity and women in leadership are fostering relationships between diversity, Christian ministry, and society (Virick & Greer, 2012). Gender differences within certain organization are classified by a variety of metaphors, that signify biases and discriminatory obstacles that hinder women in leadership (Smith et al., 2012). The purpose of Chapter 3 is to provide a detailed description of the research methodology the current study used to answer the central research and three sub questions. Described in Chapter 3 are the research methods and design the researcher used to collect and analyze the data for the current research study.

Chapter 3: Methodology

Introduction

The purpose of this qualitative case study was to explore how women perceived and overcame social, cultural, and perceptual barriers to succeed as leaders in Christian ministry. The internal, external, and self-perceived barriers that exist for women in Christian ministry leadership were explored through direct interaction with the participants (Johnson & Christensen, 2012). The phenomenon that were studied are, a) how women in leadership perceived their experiences as leaders, b) how they explained their own learned and inherent characteristics, c) why they persevered in the profession, and d) how they contended with barriers in Christian ministry within the United States.

There was plenty of literature that described female Christian ministry leaders, however, this study explored an area that has been underrepresented, i.e., how women perceive the constraints and their own leadership abilities

(Moor et al., 2015). This chapter outlined the specific problem and research questions that are under investigation. Then the methodology, research design, and population used for the study were explained in detail. The components of this chapter included the sources of data and the reliability and validity of the data to be collected. Inclusive in this chapter were the ethical considerations that were applied to each participant along with the research limitations. Upon closing of this chapter, a summary that identified key points within the chapter was transitioned into Chapter 4, which provided an explanation of data analysis and the results from the research.

Statement of the Problem

It was not known how women perceived and overcame social, cultural, and perceptual barriers to succeed as leaders in Christian ministry. This literature review included information pertaining to cultural perception of women and how historically, gender has played a pivotal role in whether or not women receive Christian Ministry

Leadership positions. The societal perception of women has been passed down through cultural teachings while misrepresenting female Christian ministry leaders (Vasavada, 2012). Women in leadership have not always been accepted due to tradition and cultural perceptions, regardless women should not eliminate their leadership assignments. (Bacha & Walker, 2013). Their behaviors have also challenged the set traditions and rituals by going beyond the norm and reaching for what they are purposed to do (Paustian-Underdahl et al., 2014).

Inclusive of cultural perception and cultural behaviors, a continued discussion of cultural barriers examined a training tool for women in leadership to gain knowledge and influence in Christian ministry (Vevere, 2014). Gender diversity in leadership examined female Christian ministry leaders who are influencing the nature of diversity and women in leadership who are fostering relationships between diversity, Christian ministry, and society (Virick & Greer, 2012). Gender differences within certain organization are classified by a variety of metaphors, that signify biases and discriminatory obstacles that hinder women in leadership (Smith et al., 2012). Exploring female Christian ministry leaders' experiences with social, cultural, and perceptual barriers provided a basis for understanding what these barriers are, and how to negate those barriers (Christian & Zippay, 2012).

According to Mento (2014), women in leadership nurture growth, and are a valuable asset to Christian leadership. This study seeks to understand how women perceive their personal obstacles in Christian leadership. Further, this research revealed the cultural, social, and perceptual barriers that women face when they seek Christian leadership positions and what some have done to overcome these barriers. The internal barriers that exist because of cultural beliefs play a vital role in leadership. The external factors of social interaction were a determining factor in what was deemed acceptable within an organization. However, the greatest challenge that is faced as a female Christian ministry leader was the self-perceived barriers that exist for women in Christian ministry leadership examined through direct interaction with the participants (Johnson & Christensen, 2012).

Examining female Christian ministry leaders' experiences with internal and external barriers that exist, because of the perception of society and culture provided a basis for understanding what these barriers are, and how to negate those barriers (Christian & Zippay, 2012). According to Mento (2014), women in leadership nurture growth, a valuable asset to Christian leadership. This study seeks to understand how women perceive their personal obstacles in Christian leadership. Furthermore, this research revealed the personal, social, and perceptual barriers that women face when they seek Christian leadership positions and what some have done to overcome these barriers. Therefore, this study provided insight on these barriers, and recommendations can be made so that women in leadership can be successful despite the barriers (Newkirk & Cooper, 2013).

Research Questions

Analyzing the experiences of women in leadership position identified and categorized the perception of their experiences. Understanding how, women in Christian leadership identified and perceived social, cultural, and self-perceived barriers fulfilled the purpose of this study. The purpose of this qualitative case study was to explore how women perceived and overcame social, cultural, and perceptual barriers to succeed as leaders in Christian ministry. The "how" question identified the steps that women can take to be successful with the current social, cultural, and perceptual barriers, which was that the perceptions of these barriers, regarding this phenomenon remain unknown. Discovering the "what" question identified and provides information unknown regarding the social, cultural, and perceptual barriers that women face when seeking leadership positions. Answering the posed "why" question delved deeper into the phenomenon by expanding on the perseverance of women to overcome barriers, furthering the study, and addressing better the purpose and problem of this study.

The qualitative methodology with a case study design makes answering these questions possible by allowing participants to describe in detail, their perceptions, accounts, and experiences with the phenomenon (Yin, 2009). The female Christian ministry leaders' experiences revealed obstacles as well as defined strategies for success in Christian ministry. The examination of their experiences identified pathways to improve societal perceptions. The phenomenon was how women in leadership perceive their experiences in Christian ministry. Women in leadership contend with internal and external barriers in Christian ministry. Female Christian ministry leaders are subject to the reality of biases, favoritism, and discrimination. Some female Christian ministry Leaders has overcome barriers. Society and culture have trained women to become effective leaders by overcoming these barriers. These barriers are largely present due to cultural perceptions and behaviors.

>R1: What social barriers do women face when they seek Christian leadership positions?

>R2: What cultural barriers do women face when they seek Christian leadership positions?

>R3: What perceptual barriers do women face when they seek Christian leadership positions?

>R4: How have women overcome social, cultural, and perceptual barriers when taking on leadership roles in Christian ministry?

The instruments used to collect the data for the qualitative case study are questionnaires, interviews, and journal field notes. The qualitative methodology with a case study design drew upon specific data to answer research questions (Isaacs, 2014). The questionnaire was structured to ask 10 women in Christian leadership roles a series of open-ended questions related to the barriers that they contend with in Christian ministry. Researcher-written interview questions and a questionnaire answered the research questions. A field-test on the interview questions and questionnaire ensured alignment, appropriateness, and validity. Questionnaires returned data on demographics, experience, job duties, training, and educational levels. The interviews were captured on NVIVO, which is a system that recorded the interview and transcribed the data as well. Open-ended questions were presented for the participants to provide an in depth response to answer what barriers exist and how their experiences are self-perceived while having the opportunity to elaborate on the answer by providing a comment/explanation.

The population consisted of women leaders in Christian ministry within the United States. The sample size was 10 females who were currently working in leadership positions. The instruments that were used to collect the data for the qualitative case study are questionnaires, interviews, and journal field notes. Permission was given by the female Christian ministry leaders who lead and/or have established a nonprofit organization. The preparation process prior to collecting data was to get approval of participants, and Institutional Review Board (IRB) approval. Along with the approvals (Appendix B), field-test (Appendix J) for the data collection instruments were tested for approval and accuracy. All data were protected by removing all personal identifiable information such as names, emails, dates, and numbers that may reference or cross-reference the participants. The researcher made all known efforts to alleviate biases, personal beliefs, judgments, partiality, impartiality, discrimination, and favoritism.

The proposal for the research was delivered to the Grand Canyon University (GCU) IRB for final authorization. Subject endorsement, the approval letter was submitted back to GCU's IRB for final approval. Following final IRB and approval, the Christian ministry leaders contributing in the study based on the criteria was sent a letter enlightening the purpose of the study. Informed consent by the principal respondents was requested. Field tests were conducted on the questionnaires and interview questions to assess alignment, appropriateness, and validity. Respondents were sent a letter by email regarding the study, which included how their confidentiality will be maintained.

This study used purposive sampling. Candidates were informed by email of their selection for participation by, informing them that participation was voluntary, resignation can occur at any time, pseudonyms were used to conceal the identity, and data were stored on a flash drive locked in a container for six years with access only given to the researcher. Questionnaires were disseminated by email first, to all participants to allow adequate time for participants to express their answers and meet the deadline for returning the questionnaire, prior to or at the time of the interviews. The participants had a deadline to return the questionnaire by email that consisted of a period of 3 days or 72 hours.

In-depth, semi-structured interviews were arranged with the participant at an agreed upon location by phone and a follow up phone call to confirm appointment. The participants were knowledgeable of the interviews lasting up to an hour in length and follow-up interviews may be needed. The researcher kept a journal that does not enclose any confidential information with the exclusion of the researcher's last name. All entries were dated, time-stamped and included only the pseudonyms of the participants, if needed.

Research Methodology

The qualitative methodology was the best approach for answering the research questions because it examines the barriers, experiences, and self-perceptions that exist for female Christian ministry leaders (Lambert & Lambert, 2012). Understanding this phenomenon was required to gain access into clarifying the perceptions of the participants. The qualitative methodology is different from numbers, frequencies, and amounts that are involved with quantitative research (Stake, 1995). Stake (1995) recommended a qualitative methodology design as a powerful narrative and investigation of a phenomenon, such as the self-perceived barriers of women in Christian leadership positions. Therefore, a qualitative case study design was used to explore how women in leadership perceive their experiences in Christian ministry. A qualitative case study provided a deeper understanding of a phenomenon through producing a deeper response to the interview questions. The case study investigated the strength of the relationship between self-identified inherent and learned characteristics of success (Stake, 1978, 1995, 1998). The qualitative methodology was the best approach for answering the research questions because it explores the barriers, experiences, and self-perceptions that exist for female Christian ministry leaders (Lambert & Lambert, 2012). Understanding this phenomenon requires the qualitative methodology to delve into participants' perceptions rather than numbers, frequencies, or amounts like that of quantitative research (Singh, 2015). The qualitative case study was chosen because the mixed-methods methodology, like quantitative research, fails to focus on the perceptions of participants, thereby will not generate an understanding of the phenomenon (Singh, 2015). Therefore, the qualitative case study methodology is essential to understanding the posed phenomenon.

The qualitative case study design was selected based on the need to explore the history of unique experiences and narrative self-perceptions of women in leadership. Identifying these barriers will uncover hindrances to their success while serving as a leader in Christian ministry (Johnson & Christensen, 2012; Stake, 2005; Yin, 2009). The qualitative case study design was chosen so that the researcher can receive data and information from more than one primary data analysis (Frost, 2011). Merriam (2009) explained that research focused on discovery, insight and understanding from the perspectives of those being studied offers the greatest promise of making significant contributions to the knowledge base and practice of education. Qualitative case study research approaches a problem of practice from a holistic perspective in order to gain an in-depth understanding of the situation and its meaning for those involved. The interest is in process rather than outcomes, in context rather than a specific variable, in discovery rather than in conformation. The case study research design is necessary for this study exploring a qualitative phenomenon. A case study will answer the "how" and "why" research questions and explain the contemporary events over time that is the phenomenon (Yin, 2009).

Research Design

The qualitative case study design discovered the history and experiences of women in leadership self-perceptions. The objective of this qualitative study was to explore how women in leadership classify and distinguish barriers in Christian ministry. The study identified the phase's female Christian ministry leaders must transition in for overcoming barriers and revealed their perceptions about their particular leadership abilities. Identifying these barriers will confiscate limitations to their success and permit for diligence, while serving as a leader in Christian ministry (Johnson & Christensen, 2012). Female Christian ministry leaders in the United States are becoming a viable component to leadership of nonprofit organizations (Fiedler, 2010).

The qualitative case study provides the researcher the chance to obtain unlimited data and information from several primary data source (Frost, 2011). The qualitative case study design additionally lets the researcher approach a phenomenon from a holistic perspective with the intent to expand an in-depth understanding of the condition and its significance to the individuals or groups involved. The focus was in the process rather than consequences, in context rather than a specific variable, in detection rather than in conformation. Merriam (2009) explained that research attentive on discovery, awareness, and understanding from the perspectives of those being studied, offers the greatest assurance of making noteworthy contributions to the knowledge base and practice of education. A case study will answer the "how" research questions and explain the modern-day events over time that was the phenomenon (Yin, 2009).

A total sample size of 10 was appropriate to establish a case and reach saturation (Yin, 2009). Qualitative case studies provide an in depth understanding of a phenomenon through manufacturing an even more intense reaction to the open-ended interview questions. The case study examined the strength of the correlation between self-identified inherent and learned characteristics of success (Stake, 1978, 1995, 1998). Stake (1995) endorsed a qualitative methodology and design as a prevailing description and analysis of a phenomenon, such as the self-perceived barriers of women in Christian leadership positions.

Therefore, case qualitative study design was used to explore how women in leadership perceive their experiences in Christian ministry. The qualitative methodology was the best approach for answering the research questions because it searched the barriers, experiences, and self-perceptions that exist for female Christian ministry leaders (Lambert & Lambert, 2012). Understanding this phenomenon was a prerequisite to advance further into expounding on the perceptions of the participants. The qualitative methodology is different from numbers, frequencies, and amounts that are involved with quantitative research (Stake, 1995).

Population and Sample Selection

The general population consisted of women leaders in Christian ministry within the United States. The sample size was 10 female Christian ministry leaders in various cities within the United States (Frost, 2011). The instruments that were used to collect the data for the qualitative case study are questionnaires, interviews, and journal field notes. Permission was given by the female Christian ministry leaders who lead and/or have established a nonprofit organization. The sample was recruited via purposive methods from midst a group of women within the United States that are in Christian leadership positions who were contacted by the researcher and asked to participate.

The case study probed the strength of the relationship between self-identified inherent and learned characteristics of success (Stake, 1978, 1995, 1998). Stake (1995) acclaimed a qualitative methodology and design as a potent narrative and inquiry of a phenomenon, such as the self-perceived barriers of women in Christian leadership positions. The qualitative methodology was the best tactic for answering the research questions because it explores the barriers, experiences, and self-perceptions that exist for female Christian ministry leaders (Lambert & Lambert, 2012). Therefore, a qualitative case study design was used to discover how women in leadership recognize their experiences in Christian ministry. Qualitative case studies provided a profounder understanding of a phenomenon through generating a deeper response to the open-ended interview questions. Understanding this phenomenon was a required condition that gives an advantage to into illuminating the perceptions of the participants. The qualitative methodology was unlike other methodologies that consist of numbers, frequencies, and amounts that are involved with quantitative research (Stake, 1995).

Along with the approvals, the field test for the data collection instruments was tested for approval and accuracy. All data were protected by removing all personal identifiable information such as names, emails, dates, and numbers that may reference or cross-reference the participants. The researcher made all known efforts to avoid biases, personal beliefs, judgments, partiality, impartiality, discrimination, and favoritism.

The population consisted of women leaders in Christian ministry within the United States. A total sample size of 10 was appropriate to comprise a case and reach saturation (Yin, 2009). The case study research design for this study was discovering a qualitative phenomenon. A case study answered the "how," "what," and "why" research questions and clarified the present events over time that was the phenomenon (Yin, 2009). Although phenomenological research receives insightful portrayals of how an individual experiences a phenomenon (Pringle et al., 2011), case studies echo real-life encounters and provides comprehensive data from open-ended interviews making case study most appropriate (Cronin, 2014; Yin, 2009). This qualitative case study required the researcher to choose the sample (Stake, 2000); strategically choosing the participants will provide a thorough understanding of the phenomenon. The instruments that were used to accumulate the data for the qualitative case study are questionnaires, open-ended interviews, and field notes that were used only for clarification by researcher during interviews. Consent was given by the female Christian ministry leaders who lead and/or have established a nonprofit organization. The preparation process prior to collecting data was to get approval of participants, and Institutional Review Board (IRB) approval. Along with the approvals, field-testing for the data collection instruments was for approval and accuracy. All data were sheltered by removing all personal identifiable information such as names, emails, dates, and numbers that may reference or cross-reference the participants. The researcher made all known efforts to lessen biases, personal beliefs, judgments, partiality, impartiality, discrimination, and favoritism.

1. The proposal for the research was provided to the Grand Canyon University (GCU) IRB for final approval.

2. Subject approval, the approval letter was submitted back to GCU's IRB for final approval.

3. Following final IRB and approval, the Christian ministry leaders participating in the study based on the criteria were sent a letter explaining the purpose of the study. Informed consent by the principal respondents was requested.

4. Field tests were conducted on the questionnaires and open-ended interview questions to assess alignment, appropriateness, and validity.

5. Respondents were sent a letter regarding the study, and was informed on how their confidentiality will be maintained. This study used purposive sampling. The population was recruited via purposive methods from among a group of women in Christian leadership positions who can be contacted by the researcher and asked to participate. The women will be current or former leaders in Christian ministry. This qualitative case study requires the researcher to choose the sample (Stake, 2000); strategically choosing the participants will provide a thorough understanding of the phenomenon.

6. Candidates were notified, by email, of their selection for participation, informed that participation was voluntary; resignation can occur at any time, pseudonyms will be used to conceal the identity, and data will be stored in a flash drive locked in a container for six years with access only given to the researcher.

7. Questionnaires were distributed by email first to all participants to allow adequate time for participants to convey their responses and meet the deadline for returning the questionnaire prior to or at the time of the interviews. The participants had a deadline to return the questionnaire by email that consisted of a period of 3 days or 72 hours.

8. In-depth, open-ended interviews were scheduled with the participant at an agreed upon location by phone and a follow up phone call to confirm appointment. The participants were informed that interviews would last up to an hour in length and follow-up interviews will be necessary with all participants in the event that new themes or questions arise from the interviews. That assured for reliability and validity to the research design.

9. The researcher also took clarifying notes during the open-ended interviews that do not contain any confidential information with the exception of the researcher's last name to review further after the interview. All entries were dated and time-stamped and included only the pseudonyms of the participants, if needed.

10. Per the Belmont Report (1979), all participants completed an informed consent ensuring the anonymity, security, and preservation of their dialogue. The participants were assigned an

identification number after the interview process. Although participation was confidential, the collection of demographic and descriptive data about each participant linked each participant with their dialogue. In accordance to the ethical principles of Belmont Report (1979), respect for persons involves a recognition, obligation, and requirement to protect a participant's personal autonomy and minimize possible risks.

Sources of Data

The instruments that were used to gather the data for this qualitative case study are questionnaires, interviews, and journal field notes. The qualitative methodology with a case study design appeals upon precise data to answer research questions (Isaacs, 2014). One important notion of the case study was triangulation. Stake (2005) defined it as "a process of using multiple perceptions to clarify meaning, verifying the repeatability of an observation or interpretation." (p. 454). This source was essential to evade fallacies. In addition, triangulation can be achieved through repetitiveness of data gathered and routine challenges to explanations. Various steps within the triangulation process are advantageous to conducting a qualitative case study.

First, the researcher should identify the theory regarding the topic. Secondly, a specific and unique phenomenon, was identified which aids in the selection of research questions. After the research questions have been developed, the researcher collects the data from interviews, questionnaires, and journal field notes. The following steps would be to organize the data by placing them in order according to categories, patterns, and themes related to the topic, which allowed for editing. The researcher then formulated triangulation of interviews, journal field notes, and questionnaires to properly transcribe and interpret.

The questionnaire was structured to ask 10 women functioning in a Christian leadership role, a series of open-ended questions related to the barriers that they contend with in Christian ministry. Researcher-written interview questions and a questionnaire answered the research questions. A field-test on the interview questions and questionnaire confirmed alignment, appropriateness, and validity. Questionnaires returned data on demographics, experience, job duties, training, and educational levels.

The interviews were captured on NVIVO, which is a system that recorded the interviews and transcribed the data by extrapolating common themes, words, and phrases from multiple sources. Once data has been gathered together under descriptive codes and thematic ideas emerged from this process with the data connected together. NVIVO adds precision to the analysis process, which allowed the researcher to carry out quick and accurate searches of a particular type and added to the validity of the results by ensuring that all instances of a particular usage were found. Open-ended questions were presented for the participants to provide in depth responses to answer what barriers exist and how their experiences are self-perceived while having the opportunity to elaborate on the answers by providing comments/explanations.

The study identified the barriers and self-perceptions of female Christian ministry leaders. The data collected from the surveys were analyzed across and within to determine if common themes and patterns exist among the participants. This purposive, qualitative case study requires the researcher to choose the sample (Stake, 2000); strategically choosing the participants provided an exhaustive understanding of the phenomenon. The responses were coded to answer the research questions, provide validity, and identify whether the female Christian ministry leaders perceive their experiences as barriers (Rabinovich & Kacen, 2013). The data results found from the open-ended interviews retained particulars for detecting the types of barriers and provided a more complete definition. Once the barriers were identified, the open-ended interview process facilitated to determine whether the female Christian ministry leaders perceive the barriers as an internal or external barrier. To collect the appropriate data, the instruments that were used are questionnaires, audio-taped open-ended interviews, and field notes. Specifically, each research question below was answered via the stated data collection instruments:

Validity

This study established validity through credibility and dependability, which are required for qualitative research. Credibility and dependability was evident in this study by removing bias, prejudice, judgments, and any preconceived notions regarding female Christian ministry leaders. Therefore, open-ended interview questions strengthened the credibility of the researcher by maintaining a neutral and objective position. The researcher attentively listened to the responses given by the female Christian ministry leaders to the open-ended questions and gained valuable insight regarding the interviewee's experiences.

Validity was captured by the chosen instruments constructed to ensure that themes and codes were measured appropriately. The responsibility was on the researcher to extract and construct the potential interview questions from the literature and theories that support the study. The instruments were used appropriately according to the standard of procedures. The researcher was the instrument used during the interview process and confirmed the validity of the study and therefore followed proper procedures. Additionally, the field test as an instrument provided validity with the expert feedback received by the participants.

The time during the interview was important because of the notes that were being taken by the researcher and the time after the interview was critical. The researcher reviewed the notes and brought them to a cohesive understanding that removed any confusion or gaps. It was also a good method to follow up with the interviewer if any questions should appear while reviewing the notes again. The time after the interview was a time of reflection and allowed the researcher to elaborate on other details that were observed. The researcher was accountable for the quality of the data and made certain it was valuable, trustworthy, and authentic.

Reliability

According to Yin (2009) reliability is the process of making sure the consistency and repeatability of the research procedures used in a case study are authentic. In order to achieve reliability, this study used triangulation to converge data collected from different sources (Yin, 2009). The sources of data included questionnaires, interviews, and journal field notes (Yin, 2009).

The data collected from the surveys were analyzed to determine if common themes and patterns exist among the participants. The responses were coded to answer the research questions, provide validity, and identify whether the female Christian ministry leaders perceive their experiences as barriers (Rabinovich & Kacen, 2013). The data results found from the interviews carefully retained details for identifying the types of barriers and provided a more detailed definition of women's perceptions regarding their experiences in Christian Ministry. Once the barriers were identified, the interview process helped to determine whether the female Christian ministry leaders perceive the barriers as an internal or external barrier. The verbal and nonverbal cues in journal notes may express similar themes, patterns, attitudes, and behaviors to determine if the barriers are internal or external.

One important concept of the case study was triangulation. According to Stake (2005) multiple perception are used to interpret, clarify, and verify information that is repeated through observation. Multiple sources are pertinent to gathering data to ensure the alignment of the study with its purpose. Additionally, multiple sources provided a substantial amount of data in order to consider for themes and patterns. The triangulation of data gleaned for this qualitative case study included information from questionnaires, audio-taped open-ended interviews, and notes (Stake, 1978, 1995, 1998; Yin, 2009). This source was essential to elude misconception. In addition, triangulation can be achieved through repetitiveness of data gathered and routine challenges to explanations. Various steps within the triangulation process are conducive to conducting a qualitative case study. First, the researcher identified the theory concerning the topic. Secondly, a specific and unique phenomenon, was identified which aided in the selection of research questions. After the research questions have been developed, the researcher collected the data from interviews, questionnaires, and journal field notes. The following steps would be to organize the data by placing them in order according to categories, patterns, and themes related to the topic, which allowed for editing. The researcher then formulated triangulation of interviews, journal field notes, and questionnaires to properly transcribe and interpret to assure reliability.

Data Collection and Management

The preparation process prior to collecting data was to get Institutional Review Board (IRB) approval, after which the participants were recruited and approval from the participants was obtained, and. The proposal for the research was provided to the Grand Canyon University (GCU) IRB for final approval. After the approval of the proposal, the approval letter was given back to GCU's IRB for final sanction. Succeeding final IRB and approval, the Christian ministry leaders participating in the study based on the standards were sent a letter providing an explanation regarding the purpose of the study. Along with the approvals, the field test for the data collection instruments was tested for approval and accuracy.

The population consisted of women leaders in Christian ministry within the United States. An email invitation was sent to the sample size of 10 females who were working in leadership positions. A request was then made for the informed consent by the principal respondents. Questionnaires were sent to the participants to be filled out and interviews were conducted with each participant. A letter was sent to the respondents with information pertaining to the maintenance of their confidentiality. Selections were made and the determinations were made aware to the candidates by email.

Additionally, candidates were also made aware that their participation was voluntary and at any time, it was their decision not to participate. Furthermore, participant's identity and data collected would remain hidden on a flash drive locked in a locked container for six years. The participants were confirmed by receiving responses from the invitations that were previously submitted. Q&A session was scheduled with participants to answer any questions or concerns that they may have. During the time of Q&A, the consent form was signed and an agreement to start the process was noted. Once the consent sign was completed by both parties the questionnaire was submitted for the participant to complete. Questionnaires were dispersed by email first to all participants to allow sufficient time for participants to deliver their responses and meet the deadline for returning the questionnaire prior to or at the time of the interviews. The researcher had a goal to return the questionnaire by email that involved a target of 3 days or 72 hours.

  Once the participant completed the questionnaire, an interview was scheduled for a date that was advantageous to both the researcher and participant. Once the interview was scheduled a reminder email with the date, time, and location was sent to the participant. Interviews were conducted and lasted approximately 30 minutes. The participants gained knowledge that interviews lasted up to an hour in length and follow-up interviews were required with all participants in the event that different themes or questions arise from the interviews. That guaranteed for reliability and validity to the research design.

Data were triangulated with the questionnaire, interview, and field notes. Data were categorized to analyze common phrases, themes, and words. The data were then placed on tables and graphs with color-coded methods and numbering system. Commonality of social, cultural, and perceptual barriers were identified as findings, which were documented, applied, and presented. The instruments that were used to collect the data for the qualitative case study are questionnaires, interviews, and journal field notes. Permission was given by the female Christian ministry leaders who lead and/or have established a nonprofit organization. All data were protected by removing all personal identifiable information such as names, emails, dates, and numbers that may reference or cross-reference the participants. The researcher made all known efforts to alleviate biases, personal beliefs, judgments, partiality, impartiality, discrimination, and favoritism.

The researcher also took clarifying notes during the open-ended interviews that did not include any personal information with the omission of the researcher's last name to review further after the interview. All records were date and time-stamped and included only the pseudonyms of the participants, if needed.

Protection and management of data. The notes are kept for six years locked in a file cabinet with a key to which only the researcher only has access. All information pertaining to the study will be stored on a flash drive locked in a container for six years. After six years, all physical information pertaining to this study will be shredded. Prior to six years, the hard copies of information will be stored in a key-locked cabinet in the key-locked office on the researcher's premises for six years. After six years, the documents will be shredded by the researcher and recycled. Interviews were audio recorded and saved on the researcher's laptop. The audio recordings will be stored in a key-locked cabinet in the researcher's key-locked home office. The tape recordings will be deleted from the audio recording device after six years and the device will be reset to factory settings.

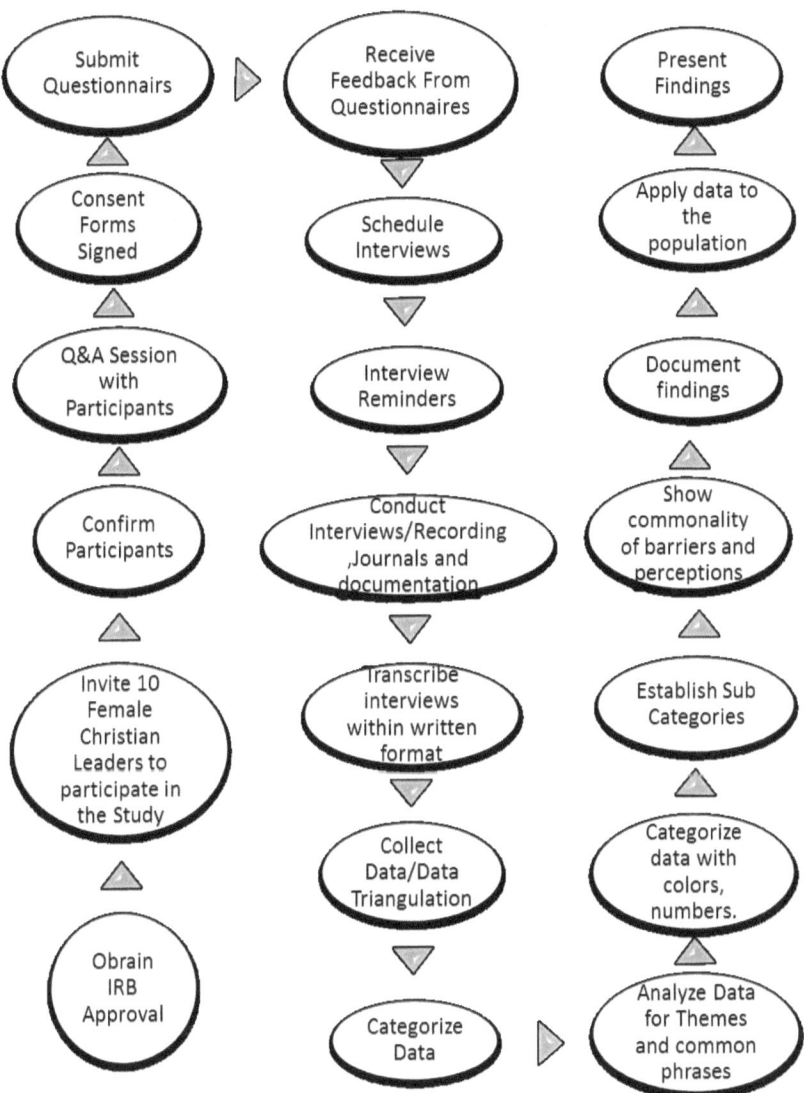

Figure 1. Research procedure.

Data Analysis Procedures

The study identified the barriers and self-perceptions of female Christian ministry leaders. This qualitative case study requires the researcher to choose the sample (Stake, 2000); strategically choosing the participants provided a thorough understanding of the phenomenon. The data collected from the surveys was analyzed across and within to determine common themes and patterns exist among the participants. One important concept of the case study was triangulation. Stake (2005) defined it as "a process of using multiple perceptions to clarify meaning and verify the repeatability of an observation or interpretation." (p. 454). Multiple sources are pertinent to gathering data to ensure the alignment of the study with its purpose. Additionally, multiple sources provided a substantial amount of data in order to consider for themes and patterns. The triangulation of data gleaned for this qualitative case study included information from questionnaires, audio-taped open-ended interviews, and notes (Stake, 1978, 1995, 1998; Yin, 2009).

This case study seeks to answer "how", "what", and "why" questions which demonstrated the need for qualitative data. The research questions in this case study were addressed by the triangulation of three data sets (questionnaires, open-ended interviews, and field notes). Case studies often use multiple sources of data to explain contemporary events and the use of triangulation enables the researcher to corroborate the research findings (Yin, 2014). According to Yin (2014), a case study "is an empirical inquiry that investigates a contemporary phenomenon, (the "case") in depth and within its real-world context" (p. 16). A qualitative case study provided the necessary data to complete this research and answer these research questions (See Table) 1:

R1: What social barriers do women face when they seek Christian leadership positions?

R2: What cultural barriers do women face when they seek Christian leadership positions?

R3: What perceptual barriers do women face when they seek Christian leadership positions?

R4: How have women overcome social, cultural, and perceptual barriers when taking on leadership roles in Christian ministry?

The relevant data that was collected was how women in leadership contended with internal and external barriers in Christian ministry. Marianne & Miemie (2014) suggested that researchers have a plan in place to manage the data and reduce it in a meaningful way. For this research, incorporating a database to gather the data for the convenience of manipulating the data into meaningful information (that is, sorting, creating queries, creating reports) was done by uploading selected documents into NVivo software. By utilizing data analysis, the researcher assigned meaning to words and sentences guided by the responses from each participant. The data were analyzed, categorized, and placed in categories. The color-coded categories that consisted of words and phrases launched developing themes that formed patterns to answer the research questions. The words, phrases, themes, and patterns provided validity, and identified that the female Christian ministry leader perceived their experiences as barriers (Rabinovich & Kacen, 2013). The data results found from the open-ended interviews carefully retained details for identifying the types of barriers and provided a more detailed definition. Once the barriers were identified, the open-ended interview process helped to determine whether the female Christian ministry leaders perceive the barriers as an internal or external barrier. These common words and phrases are what the researcher sought to find per patterns and categorizing the data from the interviews, questionnaires, and journal field notes. Several patterns were identified that included internal and external barriers, personal barriers, social barriers, and perceptual barriers.

Additionally, patterns of inherent characteristics, learned behaviors, and coping mechanisms were also identified. The patterns mean that barriers do exist in Christian ministry for female leaders, which means that women in leadership positions within Christian ministry needed to implement ways to succeed in spite of these barriers. The significance of identifying these barriers helped female Christian ministry leaders better understand and cope with a strategy to move forward and progress.

Ten face-to-face interviews were conducted with female Christian ministry leaders of non-profit organizations. The interviews consisted of 4 questions and 6 sub questions. Interviews lasted a minimum of 45 minutes to a maximum of 2 hours depending upon the individual participant and the need and wiliness to share. During the interviews, observations were noted by the researcher for the duration of the interviews. Transcribed interviews for 10 participants totaled between 20-25 pages of single spaced words and range from 2 to 3 pages per participant. During the interviews, observations were made and field notes were taken as words and phrases. Field notes were collected during the data collection on all 10 participants and each participant has one page dedicated for field notes.

The female Christian ministry leaders' experiences revealed obstacles as well as defined strategies for success in Christian ministry. Some female Christian ministry leaders have overcome barriers, which was relevant to this study. Society and culture have trained women to become effective leaders by overcoming these barriers. Female Christian ministry leaders are subject to the relevant reality of biases, favoritism, and discrimination. These barriers are largely present due to cultural perceptions and behaviors. Analyzing the experiences of women in leadership position identified and categorized the perception of their experiences. The examination of their experiences identified passageways to improve societal perceptions. The purpose of this qualitative case study was to explore how women perceived and overcame social, cultural, and perceptual barriers to succeed as leaders in Christian ministry (Scott, 2010). Secondly, to examine what processes women have taken to overcome these barriers (Michailidis et al., 2012).

Thirdly, identify inherent and learned characteristics necessary for Christian leadership (Wienclaw, 2015)

The researcher managed the collected data through organizing the data collected from interviews, questionnaires, and journal field notes. The following steps would be to organize the data by placing it in order according to categories, patterns, and themes related to the topic, which allowed for editing. The researcher then formulated triangulation of interviews, journal field notes, and questionnaires to properly transcribe and interpret. The questionnaire was structured to ask 10 women in Christian leadership roles a series of open-ended questions related to the barriers that they contended with in Christian ministry. Researcher-written interview questions and a questionnaire answered the research questions. A field-test on the interview questions and questionnaire ensured alignment, appropriateness, and validity. Questionnaires returned data on demographics, experience, job duties, training, and educational levels. The interviews were captured on

NVIVO, which was a system that recorded the interview and transcribed the data as well. Open-ended questions were presented for the participants to provide in depth responses to answer what barriers exist and how their experiences were self-perceived while having the opportunity to elaborate on the answers by providing comments/explanations.

The responses were color coded by words, phrases, themes, and patterns to answer the research questions, provide validity, and identify whether the female Christian ministry leader perceived their experiences as barriers (Rabinovich & Kacen, 2013). The data results found from the open-ended interviews carefully retained details for identifying the types of barriers and provided a more detailed definition. Once the barriers were identified, the open-ended interview process helped to determine whether the female Christian ministry leaders perceive the barriers as an internal or external barrier.

Stake (1995) recommended a qualitative methodology design as an influential narrative and investigation of a phenomenon, such as the self-perceived barriers of women in Christian leadership positions. Therefore, case qualitative study design was used to explore how women in leadership perceive their familiarities in Christian ministry. Qualitative case studies provided a deeper understanding of a phenomenon through manufacturing a deeper response to the open-ended interview questions. The case study investigated the potency of the relationship between self-identified inherent and learned characteristics of success (Stake, 1978, 1995, 1998). The qualitative methodology was the best approach for answering the research questions because it scrutinizes the barriers, experiences, and self-perceptions that exist for female Christian ministry leaders (Lambert & Lambert, 2012). Understanding this phenomenon was indeed a benefit for attaining access into simplifying the perceptions of the participants. The qualitative methodology is not the same as amounts, regularities, and volumes that are involved with quantitative research (Stake, 1995).

To collect the appropriate data, the instruments that were used are questionnaires, audio-taped open-ended interviews, and field notes. Specifically, each research question below was answered via the stated data collection instruments. Along with the approvals, the field-test process, for the data assembly instruments were tested for support and exactness. All data were protected by confiscating all personal recognizable information such as names, emails, dates, and numbers that may reference or cross-reference the participants. The researcher made all known efforts to lessen biases, personal beliefs, judgments, partiality, impartiality, discrimination, and favoritism.

Ethical Considerations

Participants completed an informed consent form to ensure that their information was secured and preserved with a personalized identifiable number. Although all participants are anonymous, the collection of data included demographics and descriptive data regarding all participants, which referenced each participant with their information. The reference was included on the informed consent form. The personalized identifiable numbers were created to reduce the hardship of identification of the participant but anonymity was maintained. It was the option of the participant to withdraw at any time. All information was stored on a flash drive locked in a container for six years, access only given to researcher. The data was stored on a flash drive locked in a container. The study did not display any partiality toward the participants based on sex, race, ethnicity, or other factors (Ryan et al., 2011).

Several steps were taken to ensure that it was an ethical study. This researcher acquired GCU IRB approval and informed consent from the principal on each participant. Participants were notified that participation was voluntary, and they could withdraw at any time; pseudonyms were assigned; participants were informed that consent documents and all hard copy documents will remain, for six years, in a key-locked filing cabinet on the researcher's premises with the key stored in the researcher's desk drawer kept in a key-locked office; and electronic information was stored on a on a flash drive locked in a container that will remain on the researcher's premises in the locked office at all times.

Participants were apportioned a numeric credential following the interview process. Additionally, participants completed an informed consent form affirming discretion of demographic information. Per the Belmont Report (1979), the disguise, welfare, and protection of the participant's exchanging information were of extreme prominence. Although participation was trustworthy, the collection of demographic and descriptive data regarding each participant jeopardizes the association of individual experiences. In accordance to the ethical principles of Belmont Report (1979), respect for the participants comprises a gratitude and stipulation to shield an individual's information and perchance exclude greater risk.

Limitations and Delimitations

One limitation was being dependent upon non-numerical data. Secondly, another limitation of a qualitative case study was the flexibility. The researcher has the flexibility to determine the appropriate questions, but if the inappropriate question was asked, the participant may provide unwanted calculations of their experiences, which has the probability of skewing the desired results. Thirdly, the described experiences could very well be painful or something that the participant was not ready to face and the participant could become offended or defensive. The fourth limitation was accurate memory regarding the experiences and describing old feelings that have been covered or previously dealt with. The participants were able to give accounts of their experiences but there could be limitations of distorted perceptions. Lastly, limitations of personal assumption the researcher brought to the study, because the researcher understands the barriers and experiences that female Christian ministry leader's face.

Delimitations include the chosen participants of the study, as each participant was a female Christian ministry leader, of a nonprofit organization, and has had or was having life experiences of the phenomenon to share in the interview. Because the female Christian ministry leaders are still experiences some barriers the researcher must be sensitive to the nature of the study and provide ways of comfort. The researcher kept a jovial disposition with a smile during the interview process. The researcher brought out elements of learning through the shared experiences and identified ways that it has strengthened the participants. Although the participants may have felt sad and shed, some tears the researcher reminded them of how far they have come and the growth that was evident. Another, delimitation to the study was the location of the participants. The 10 participants chosen to participate in the research study were female Christian ministry leaders in various types of non-profit organizations in different cities and states.

Delimitations were also based on what the researcher did not do during the study. The researcher did not pass judgment or pretend to know exactly how the participant felt. However, the researcher attempted to understand and identify as a woman, as a leader with the current societal and cultural barriers. The literature reviewed for this study pertained to the barriers that women face as a female leader in Christian ministry in a non-profit organization. The phenomenon that was studied was how women in leadership perceived their experiences as leaders, how they explained their own learned and inherent characteristics, why they persevered in the profession, and how they contended with barriers in Christian ministry within the United States. Other research topics were excluded to avoid clouding the focus of the study. The researcher did not use previously constructed interviews or questionnaires, as these data collection methods were not designed for the same purpose of the study.

Summary

In 1977, Greenleaf's Servant Leadership theory proposed a model based primarily on helping others to grow as individuals and within the community (Kemp, 2016). Servant leadership was important to this study, because serving others is not gender specific and provides a foundational standard for female Christian ministry leader to serve others regardless of gender barriers (Berger, 2014). The researcher explored the personal, social, and perceptual barriers that female Christian ministry leaders face in Christian ministry. It identified inherent and learned characteristics necessary for Christian leadership. Servant leadership theory provided a base for understanding this phenomenon. Additionally, inclusive leadership provided a prospective that included diverse perceptions, but with the need to find and understand relatable common places to enhance the well-being of individuals, groups, and organizations (Jaworski, 2012). Inclusive leadership was important to female Christian ministry leaders, because there is a need to find a common place and remove barriers (Tidball, 2012). Inclusive leadership comprehends the need for diverse cultures and promotes ways to increase acceptance while broadening perspectives. Inclusive leadership distributes power and mutual respect so that one group or individual is not in total control (Beaty & Davis, 2012).

It was not known how women leaders in Christian ministry perceived and overcame social, cultural, and perceptual barriers to succeed as leaders in Christian ministry. Examining female Christian ministry leaders' experiences with internal and external barriers provided a basis for understanding what these barriers are, and how to negate those barriers (Christian & Zippay, 2012). According to Mento (2014), women in leadership nurture growth, a valuable asset to Christian leadership. This study seeks to understand how women perceive their personal obstacles in Christian leadership. Furthermore, this research revealed the personal, social, and perceptual barriers that women face when they seek Christian leadership positions and what some have done to overcome these barriers. It also identified inherent and learned characteristics necessary for Christian leadership. Therefore, this study provided insight and strategy on these barriers. A strategy was determined as to how women in leadership can be successful despite the barriers (Newkirk & Cooper, 2013).

Stake (1995) recommended a qualitative methodology design as a powerful narrative and investigation of a phenomenon, such as the self-perceived barriers of women in Christian leadership positions. Therefore, a case study design was used to examine how women in leadership perceive their experiences in Christian ministry. Female Christian ministry leaders in the United States are becoming a sustainable element to leadership of nonprofit organizations (Fiedler, 2010). The goal of this qualitative study was to examine how women in leadership identify and perceive barriers in Christian ministry and what are the steps for women in leadership to overcome barriers in Christian ministry as well as reveal their perceptions about their own leadership qualities and provide an understanding of what causes them to persevere in this profession. The qualitative case study design was selected based on the need to examine the history of unique experiences and narrative self-perceptions of women in leadership. Identifying these barriers removed hindrances to their success while serving as a leader in Christian ministry (Johnson & Christensen, 2012).

The phenomenon studied was how women in leadership perceive their experiences as leaders, how they explain their own learned and inherent characteristics, why they persevere in this profession, and how they contend with barriers in Christian ministry within the United States. The instruments that were used to collect the data for the qualitative case study are questionnaires, interviews, and filed notes. The qualitative methodology with a case study design drew upon specific data to answer research questions (Isaacs, 2014). The questionnaire was structured to ask 10 women in Christian leadership roles a series of open-ended questions related to the barriers that they contend with in Christian ministry. Researcher-written interview questions and a questionnaire answered the research questions.

A field-test on the interview questions and questionnaire ensured alignment, appropriateness, and validity. Questionnaires returned data on demographics, experience, job duties, training, and educational levels. The interviews were captured on NVIVO, which is a system that recorded the interview and transcribed the data as well. The researcher reported the results of this qualitative case study in the oncoming chapter, Chapter 4. In this chapter, the researcher will share the transcripts of the interviews, as well as, the analysis of the data to relay the meanings of the self-perceptions and experiences of the participants. Chapter 4 will also explain learned and inherent characteristics of female Christian ministry leaders in addition to how perseverance leads to success. The results received will be synthesized by themes, codes, comparison, and summarization.

Chapter 4: Data Analysis and Results

Introduction

Detailed in Chapter 4 is an analysis of questionnaires, interviews, and journal field notes of 10 qualified leaders that were purposively selected because of the leadership positions that they currently held at the time data were collected. It was not known how women perceived and overcame social, cultural, and perceptual barriers to succeed as leaders in Christian ministry. The purpose of this qualitative case study was to explore how women perceived and overcame social, cultural, and perceptual barriers to succeed as leaders in Christian ministry. Chapter 4 provides the data collected and analyzed from the interviews that were conducted with 10 female Christian ministry leaders within a nonprofit organization in the United States to determine common themes. Themes and codes were identified, from the interviews, and then reexamined to verify recognizable patterns and categories. From the results of the themes, patterns were established. The research questions were answered with the data collected from the interviews, questionnaires, and journal field notes. The qualitative methodology was the best approach for answering the research questions because it explores the barriers, experiences, and self-perceptions that exist for female Christian ministry leaders (Lambert & Lambert, 2012). A qualitative methodology was recommended for an examination of barriers of women in Christian leadership positions and their perceived experiences as a phenomenon (Merriam, 2009).

To collect the appropriate data, the instruments that were used were questionnaires, audio-taped open-ended interviews, and field notes. Specifically, each research question below has been answered via an analysis the stated data collection instruments:

R1: What social barriers do women face when they seek Christian leadership positions?

R2: What cultural barriers do women face when they seek Christian leadership positions?

R3: What perceptual barriers do women face when they seek Christian leadership positions?

R4: How have women overcome social, cultural, and perceptual barriers when taking on leadership roles in Christian ministry?

Descriptive Data

The demographic information collected from the questionnaires consisted of the participants' years of experience and years of education or degree. The demographic information provided insight that elaborated on the experiences of 10 qualified women in Christian ministry. The first 3 questions of the questionnaire provided detailed demographical information that provided the following results. Table includes the years of experience and level of education completed. Transcribed interviews for 10 participants totaled 22 pages of single spaced words and ranges from 2 to 3 pages per participant. Field notes were written on all 10 participants and each participant has one page dedicated for field notes.

Table 1

Participants' Demographics

Participants	College Degree	Years of Leadership Experience
Participant 1	Bachelor's Degree	3-5 years of experience
Participant 2	2 years of college	10 years or more
Participant 3	Bachelor's Degree	1 to 3 years of experience
Participant 4	Master's Degree	3 - years of experience
Participant 5	Bachelor's Degree	3-5 years of experience
Participant 6	Master's Degree	10 years or more
Participant 7	Master's Degree	10 years or more
Participant 8	1 year of College	1 to 3 years of experience
Participant 9	3 years of College	1 to 3 years of experience
Participant 10	Bachelor's Degree	1 to 3 years of experience

Table 2

Participants' Positions in Christian Ministry

Participants	Position	Worked or Currently Working
Participant 1	Executive Administration	Currently Working
Participant 2	Women's Ministry	Currently Working
Participant 3	Pastor's Wife	Currently Working
Participant 4	Community Advocate	Currently Working
Participant 5	Ministry Leader	Currently Working
Participant 6	Pastor's Wife	Currently Working
Participant 7	Women's Ministry	Currently Working
Participant 8	Community Outreach	Currently Working
Participant 9	Pastor's Wife	Currently Working
Participant 10	Community Liaison	Currently Working

The data collection process started with an invitational email to 15 women in leadership positions for nonprofit organizations. After receiving an acceptance, email from the participants a follow up phone call was done for confirmation. Of the 15, only 10 accepted, 3 did not respond, and 2 decided not to participate.

Interviews took place at a home location or a private public location that was feasible for the participants. The overall goal was for the participant to feel comfortable to share. Providing a safe and private environment was key to collaboration between the participant and the researcher. All of the interviews conducted were face-to-face and included additional information of participant's behavior and expressions.

According to Cairney and St Denny (2015), a qualitative interview process transpired when the researcher questioned the participant with open-ended questions and the interview was recorded. Participants for the current study were presented 4 open-ended questions (See Appendix E).

Probing questions were used to gain clarity and address some topics that were stated. All interviews were audio taped. Journal field notes were taken regarding the non-verbal behaviors that were present. The 10 participants were coded using Female Leader 1, Female Leader 2, Female Leader 3, etc. The interviews lasted a minimum of 45 minutes to a maximum of 2 hours.

The responses from the interviews were transcribed and reviewed to the audio tape for verification and accuracy. The transcribed interview responses were entered into NVivo 10® software, which is a program used by the researcher to organize raw data, including interviews, questionnaires, and journal field notes. The software also helps determine common codes in specific categories. The following information consists of the common themes, demographic information, and findings. The initial three questions engaged with the participants to collect demographic information and the remaining interview questions, the participants described personal experiences as a female leader in Christian ministry.

Table 3

Data Summary

	Questionnaire Data	# Pages of Field notes, single spaced	Duration of Interviews	#Transcribed Interview Pages, Single spaced
Participant 1	3	.5	30 min	2
Participant 2	2	.25	30 min	1.5
Participant 3	3	.5	30 min	2
Participant 4	2	.5	30 min	2
Participant 5	3	.25	35 min	3
Participant 6	3	.25	30 min	2
Participant 7	2	.25	35 min	2
Participant 8	3	.25	30 min	3
Participant 9	2	.25	30 min	3
Participant 10	2	.25	30 min	1.5
Total	25 pages	3.25	5 hours, 10 minutes	22 pages

The attitudes, behaviors, and dispositions based on the researcher's observations are displayed in Appendix J. The field notes captured the overall disposition of the participant by taking note of the body language, voice tone, and facial expressions when certain questions were asked and specific topics were discussed. The journal field notes captured areas of sensitivity and noted what phase the participant was in regarding the topic. The phases included a sense of closure where the participant had moved on and it was easy to discuss, the participant was still, offended regarding the subject, and has not been able to move past the experience, or the participants saw it as a learning experience to further their own vision, purpose, passion in life. Some participants expressed a sense of optimism, pessimism, or melancholy. The participants were all in different phases regarding their experiences which increased the awareness of how women perceive and overcome social, cultural and perceptual barriers to succeed as leaders in Christian ministry.

Appendix K shows the experiences of the participants, steps that the participants have taken to overcome, and the participant's collaborative relationship thoughts taken from the questionnaire. The questionnaire captured the participants own words regarding their experiences of social, cultural, and perceptual barriers. Some participants expressed that issues with barriers seemingly are getting better and there are steps to help female Christian ministry leaders succeed, but not all participants have engaged in the steps. The questionnaire captured areas of need such as collaborative relationships and mentorship that was thought to be a tool that would increase the success of female Christian ministry leaders. The questionnaire revealed the participants using reading the bible, prayer, and meditation as their focus for overcoming barriers and desired the support from other female Christian ministry leaders as a way to overcome and be successful. Some participants expressed the need for going being the four walls of the church as a way of overcoming barriers because it places their focus on the needs of others and not on themselves. The participants each had their own way of describing their experiences just as their steps to succeed and overcome. However, each participant found ways to endure.

Data Analysis Procedures

Ten face-to-face interviews were conducted with female Christian ministry leaders of non-profit organizations. The interviews consisted of 4 questions and 6 sub questions. Interviews lasted a minimum of 30 minutes to a maximum of 35 minutes depending upon the individual participant and the need and willingness to share. During the interviews, journal field notes were taken to document the observations by the researcher for the duration of the interviews. The questionnaires consisted of 20 questions that were provided to the participants prior to the schedule interviews. Questionnaires returned data on demographics, experience, job duties, training, and educational levels. This qualitative case study included data from interviews, questionnaires, and journal field notes that is significant to the roles of women in Christian leadership. The present study was guided by these research questions:

R1: What social barriers do women face when they seek Christian leadership positions?

R2: What cultural barriers do women face when they seek Christian leadership positions?

R3: What perceptual barriers do women face when they seek Christian leadership positions?

R4: How have women overcome social, cultural, and perceptual barriers when taking on leadership roles in Christian ministry?

Data analysis approach. A thematic analysis of interviews, questionnaires, and journal field notes assisted in understanding the phenomenon under investigation. Thematic analysis is a method for examining themes and patterns found in documents and interpreting the artifacts in an unobtrusive and nonreactive manner (Swinth, Tomlin, & Luthman, 2015). Thematic analysis of collected evidence allows the researcher to determine where the emphasis lies (Swinth et al., 2015).

The specific qualitative analysis utilized was the thematic analysis with an inductive approach, as described by Mayring (2000). Thematic analysis is the procedure for the categorization of verbal or behavioral data for the purpose of classification, summarization, and tabulation. The content was analyzed on a descriptive level that describes and summarizes data for patterns to emerge. The analysis that was useful for this study is conceptual analysis. Conceptual analysis can be thought of as establishing the existence and frequency of concepts most often represented by words and phrases in a text. Analysis was conducted on interviews, questionnaires, and journal field notes. The data was coded, patterns were established, and patterns were clustered into categories, which developed themes. The words, phrases, patterns, and themes were examined using a method known as conceptual analysis.

The steps in the analysis are as follows.

1. Review the transcripts and make notes of relevant descriptive information.

2. Examine the notes previously made, identify, and code frequently used words or phrases.

3. Analyze the coded data list of frequently used words and phrases to identify patterns that can be clustered into categories.

4. Review the categories to determine its relevance and see if there are some that can be merged.

5. Identify the categories that can be established as Themes.

Preparation of data. Data collected from the participants were transcribed by the researcher and entered into NVivo 10 ® software. The transcripts were uploaded to NVivo to support analysis process. Each of the transcripts were linked to the participant. The NVivo software was used to code each individual participant's transcribed interview. The frequently used words and phrases referenced in Figure 2 were noted according to the observations of the researcher. The NVivo software allowed the researcher to code the data in a systematic method; however, the researcher's own observation and insight remained the key factors in analyzing the data. The coding process, including the use of words and definition of the words, was developed by the researcher based on the researcher's understanding of the words, conveyed experiences, and the perspective of how the words were articulated by the participants.

Figure 2. Represents common words and phrases by occurrences per word, phrase, theme, and code.

Analysis of data. The analysis of data took place in phases. The steps the researcher took are outlined below.

Review of all data sources. The interview and questionnaire data were first separated by the researcher of the individual participant and an initial analysis using hand coding of each participants' responses was conducted. The researcher used conceptual analysis, which is a type of analysis for analyzing and coding data. The researcher then was able to compare, conceptualize, and place the data into categories. Each transcript from the individual interviews and questionnaires were printed and carefully reviewed by the researcher line by line to identify patterns. The researcher proceeded with highlighting and making notes of key words and phrases from the transcripts during the analysis, and hand coded the relevant responses that answered the open-ended questions. The hand coding from the researcher and the conceptual analytic coding method allowed the researcher to prepare for NVivo software coding.

The interviews were cross-referenced with the questionnaire for each participate to if there was some corresponding data that could add to the common words or phrases. During the cross-reference between the interview data and the questionnaires there were other similar common words and phrases that were identified and could be used later in the analysis process in NVivo for a text search query.

Hand coding of data. To answer the research questions, the list of hand codes that were developed from the analysis of the transcripts of the interviews and questionnaires were evaluated based on their similarities with each other. The hand codes that were not related to the research questions were removed from the final list. The researcher reviewed the coded data to ensure accurate representation and understanding of the phenomenon. Once the researcher has determined the frequently used words, phrases, categories, and patterns that are relevant and valid each participant's responses were individually hand coded and then integrated within the group of female Christian ministry leaders. The hand-coded responses from the integrated group is captured on a chart that is colored coded to demonstrate the frequency within the group.

Coding process. The coding process, including the use of words and definition of the words, was developed by the researcher based on the researcher's understanding of the words, conveyed experiences, and the perspective of how the words were articulated by the participants. The coding process, including the use of words and definition of the words, was developed by the researcher based on the researcher understands of the words, conveyed experiences, and the perspective of how the words were articulated by the participants. The interviews were cross-referenced with the questionnaire for each participate to if there was some corresponding data that could add to the common words or phrases. During the cross-reference between the interview data and the questionnaires there were other similar common words and phrases that were identified and could be used in NVivo for a text search query. To answer the research questions, the list of hand codes that were observed from the analysis of the transcripts of the interviews and questionnaires were evaluated based on their similarities with each other. The hand codes that were not related to the research questions were removed from the final list. The researcher reviewed the coded data to ensure accurate representation and understanding of the phenomenon. Analyzed data were reviewed to make certain that the patterns, categories, and themes were plainly stated by the participants.

Coding using NVivo. The transcripts were uploaded to NVivo to enhance the data retrieval and analysis process. Each of the transcripts were linked to the participant. The NVivo software was used to code each individual participant's transcribed interview. The frequently used words and phrases were noted according to the observations of the researcher. The NVivo software allowed the researcher to code the data in a systematic method; however, the researcher's own observation and insight remained the key factors in analyzing the data. The transcripts were uploaded to NVivo to enhance the data retrieval and analysis process. Each of the transcripts were linked to the participant. The NVivo software was used to code each individual participant's transcribed interview. The frequently used words and phrases were noted according to the observations of the researcher.

Once the initial hand coding was complete, the research began to assign those codes as "nodes" within the NVivo software program. The inductive approach was used in analyzing the emergent data and categorize the relevant information into groups or categories. The initial coding was to determine how many participants described their experiences using the same words. The initial coding was for the frequency of participants. The second coding process was to determine the frequency of words and phrases by cross-referencing the interviews and questionnaires, which was established by NVivo. The color red category was identified by the researcher as the category that had the maximum or 10 out of 10 most common words mentioned by all participants across and within the questionnaire, interview, and journal field notes. Green was the next category that identified by the researcher words that were mentioned by more than half of the participants or 5 out of 10 participants across and within the questionnaire, interview, and journal field notes. Yellow category was for the minimum or 2 out of 4 words mentioned by participants across and within the questionnaire, interview, and journal field notes. Common phrases identified from the participants as they talked about their experiences during the interview were extrapolated across and within the questionnaire and journal field notes. All responses from each participant were analyzed, categorized, and placed in categories. The color-coded categories that consisted of words and phrases launched into developing patterns that were formed into categories, which eventually identified themes to answer the research questions. The words, phrases, patterns, categories, and themes provided validity, and identified that the female

Christian ministry leader perceived their experiences as barriers (Rabinovich & Kacen, 2013).

Frequency query. The NVivo query that best fit the study in order to answer the research questions was the word frequency query. The word frequency query identified references of common words, themes, and patterns from several sources. The sources used were the individual participant, group of participants, interview data, questionnaire data, and identified common words and phrases that were previously observed and identified by the researcher. The word frequency query report was exported in an excel format that identified how many times the sources identified the word and how many times the words were referenced.

Once the researcher was able to confirm the frequently used words and phrases with the hand-coded analysis previously completed a report by NVivo was exported allowing the researcher to take a step further and narrow the frequently used words and phrases to each participants. There were 10 participants and each frequently used word and phrase was numerically identified and matched to each participant. Because there were 10 participants the researcher used a color-coding scale from 1-10.

Thematic analysis. The researcher analyzed the data using the analytic method by Mayring (2000) and five themes emerged. The five common themes resulted throughout the interview process were: (a) Female Perception of Leadership (b) Characteristics of Female Leadership (c) Internal and External Barriers (d) Leadership Momentum (e) Coping Mechanisms. The responses that included certain words, phrases, and thoughts were colored coded by the researcher using the color red, green, and yellow to identify the different categories.

The first theme that was selected from hand coded from the researcher's analysis emerged from was the word perception. The researcher observed and identified perceptual barriers and perceived internal barriers as two categories that the hand coded frequently used words can be placed. Perceptual barriers were observed by the researcher as the outcome or reason for perceived internal barriers. Additionally, observed among the frequently used hand coded words were anger, self-blame, settling, adopting, grudge, and blaming others. An extended observation from the researcher was that the perception of the female Christian ministry leaders had been altered. The continued analysis by the researcher demonstrated frequently used words as insecure, intimidation, discouraged, and doubt as the perceived internal barriers that female Christian ministry leaders are facing. The researcher observed that the highest frequently used hand coded words in each category for perceived internal barriers and perceptual barriers were settling, adopting, self-blame, insecurity, and intimidation. These frequently used words developed patterns and were placed into categories that materialized the theme of female perceptions of leadership. The researcher observed that the perceptions changed due to the internal and external barriers that female Christian ministry leaders have faced.

Table 4

Codes for Female Perceptions of Leadership

Key Words and Phrases	Initial Category	Example from Transcript Including Source	Initial Themes
Anger	Perceptual Barriers	I was angry and wanted to revert. (Participant 4)	Female Perception of Leadership
Blame Others	Perceptual Barriers	I blame it on culture, society, and traditional baggage. (Participant 1)	Female Perception of Leadership
Grudge	Perceptual Barriers	I felt tricked. (Participant 4)	Female Perception of Leadership
Self-Blame	Perceptual Barriers	I blame myself. (Participant 3)	Female Perception of Leadership
Self-Sabotage	Perceptual Barriers	I lost my effectiveness because I was so drained from everyone else's needs. (Participant 9)	Female Perception of Leadership
Settling-Adopting	Perceptual Barriers	Woman in leadership you have to get permission. (Participant 1)	Female Perception of Leadership
Insecure	Perceived Internal Barriers	I have to keep encouraging myself because I would rather sit in the back and support others	Female Perception of Leadership

		instead of being out in front. (Participant 8)	
Intimidation	Perceived Internal Barriers	I have barriers from other women in ministry, intimidation. (Participant 1)	Female Perception of Leadership
discouraged	Perceived Internal Barriers	I stopped and retreated because people expect you to be consistent and committed no matter what. (Participant 9)	Female Perception of Leadership
Doubt	Perceived Internal Barriers	There are still denominations that will not fully receive women. (Participant 9)	Female Perception of Leadership

The second theme to emerge was female perception of leadership, and thirdly coping mechanisms was the characteristics of female leaders. The frequently used hand coded words that were observed by the researcher was commitment, dedication, accountability, determination, and sacrificial. The previously mentioned words were analyzed by the researcher as a description of the participants' responses in spite of the barriers faced. The frequently used words were hand coded into two categories, which are inherent characteristics and learned characteristics. Inherent characteristics emerged from what the researcher observed to be an essentials element for leadership. The frequently used words hand coded were fearless, motivated, relentless, strengthened, and unstoppable which were also observed by the researcher. Learned characteristics were analyzed as essential characteristics for enduring the barriers that female Christian ministry leaders face. These frequently used words developed patterns and were placed into categories that materialized the theme characteristics of female leadership, which emerged from the analysis of the researcher.

Table 5

Codes for Characteristics of Female Leadership

Key Words and Phrases	Initial Category	Example from Transcript Including Source	Initial Themes
Commitment	Inherent Characteristics	Remaining faithful to God as a single female in leadership. (Participant 4)	Characteristics of Female Leaders

Key Words and Phrases	Initial Category	Example from Transcript Including Source	Initial Themes
Dedication	Inherent Characteristics	Even when we are hurt, disappointed, and feel rejected we must remain steadfast and in position. (Participant 5)	Characteristics of Female Leaders
Accountability	Inherent Characteristics	When God gives you something to do, you move on it regardless. (Participant 6)	Characteristics of Female Leaders
Responsibility	Inherent Characteristics	We are still responsible for doing what He called us to do. (Participant 2)	Characteristics of Female Leaders
Determined	Inherent Characteristics	I am determined not to let Him down, because He has never failed me. (Participant 8)	Characteristics of Female Leaders
Sacrificial	Inherent Characteristics	I have not seen the benefits of the sacrifice. (Participant 10)	Characteristics of Female Leaders
Fearless	Inherent Characteristics	I get fearless and unstoppable because I remember the things that God has brought me	Characteristics of Female Leaders

Key Words and Phrases	Initial Category	Example from Transcript Including Source	Initial Themes
		through (Participant 2)	
Motivated	Inherent Characteristics	I am motivated because the opposition should have killed me. (Participant 4)	Characteristics of Female Leaders
Relentless	Inherent Characteristics	I am relentless. (Participant 9)	Characteristics of Female Leaders
Strengthened	Inherent Characteristics	It strengthens me to fight. (Participant 2)	Characteristics of Female Leaders
Unstoppable	Inherent Characteristics	I am unstoppable because I remember the things that God has brought me through. (Participant 2)	Characteristics of Female Leaders
Settling	Learned Characteristics	God was telling me to get it done prior to a certain time but I was waiting on approval from male leadership. (Participant 3)	Characteristics of Female Leaders
Altering	Learned Characteristics	I just wanted to be myself without altering who God created me to	Characteristics of Female Leaders

Key Words and Phrases	Initial Category	Example from Transcript Including Source	Initial Themes
		be. (Participant 8)	
Revising	Learned Characteristics	I felt the need to revise myself. (Participant 8)	Characteristics of Female Leaders
Adopting	Learned Characteristics	I struggle with separating my relationship and my love for God and my dislike for the church. (Participant 4)	Characteristics of Female Leaders
Inferiority	Learned Characteristics	Women or wives are not considered equal in ministry. (Participant 4)	Characteristics of Female Leaders

The third theme identified as the researcher continued was internal and external barriers that emerged from the researcher analyzing the responses were emotional, physical, psychological, and spiritual barriers, which were hand coded in the internal barriers category. The researcher observed that emotional and psychological barriers were referenced the most. The researcher similarly analyzed the external barriers category and observed words as acceptance, approval, disadvantage, lack of support, and protocol, which were hand coded in the second category of external barriers. The researcher also observed that lack of support and protocol were referenced the most for the category of external barriers are. The researcher identified patterns of the word perception. The researcher observed and identified two categories, perceptual barriers and perceived internal barriers. Perceptual barriers were observed by the researcher as the outcome or reason for perceived internal barriers. Additionally observed among the frequently used hand coded words were anger, self-blame, settling, adopting, grudge, and blaming others. An extended observation from the researcher was that the perception of the female Christian ministry leaders had been altered. The continued analysis by the researcher demonstrated frequently used words as insecure, intimidation, discouraged, and doubt as the perceived internal barriers that female Christian ministry leaders are facing. The researcher observed that the highest frequently used hand coded words in each category for perceived internal barriers and perceptual barriers were settling, adopting, self-blame, insecurity, and intimidation.

Table 6

Codes for Internal and External Barriers

Key Words and Phrases	Initial Code	Example from Transcript Including Source	Initial Themes
Disdain For Leadership	Social Barriers	I am not pleased with what I see with the church and how we operate how we represent God in the world. (Participant 4)	External Barriers
Routine Rituals	Social Barriers	There are so many rituals, traditions, and obligations that you have to consider prior to obeying what God want you to do. (Participant 2)	External Barriers
Traditions	Social Barriers	Men are intimidated because it is something that is not traditionally accepted. (Participant 10)	External Barriers
Belittled	Perceived Barriers	It makes me feel less than even though you know that you are not. (Participant 10)	Internal Barriers
Intimidation	Perceived Barriers	Men are intimidated because it is something that is not traditionally accepted. A subtle action is taken toward you because you are a woman. (Participant 10)	Internal Barriers
Cautious	Perceived Barriers	Whether they think God gave it to you or not you still follow through with it. (Participant 6)	Internal Barriers
Discouraged	Perceived Barriers	Even when we are hurt, disappointed, and feel rejected we must remain	Internal Barriers

Key Words and Phrases	Initial Code	Example from Transcript Including Source	Initial Themes
		steadfast and in position. (Participant 5)	
Disobedience	Perceived Barriers	Wanting to be obedient to God but dealing with the realm of the church. (Participant 4)	Internal Barriers
Doubt	Perceived Barriers	It makes me feel like I have not been walking in what God wanted me to do. (Participant 9)	Internal Barriers
Expectancy	Perceived Barriers	It is my expectation to walk into what I am called to do. (Participant 9)	Internal Barriers
Forsaken	Perceived Barriers	It is hurtful that when you do obey you are reprimanded for not obeying man. (Participant 2)	Internal Barriers
Insecurity	Perceived Barriers	I deal with my own self-insecurities prior to even meeting face to face with those that are imposed upon me from external sources. (Participant 8)	Internal Barriers
Weary	Perceived Barriers	After coming against it so long you start succumb to it or submit to you or you digress. (Participant 10)	Internal Barriers

The fourth theme to emerge from the analysis of the researcher was dealing with the current view from a female Christian ministry leader. The researcher analyzed frequently used words were expanded vision, optimistic, pessimistic, and hopeful. With the analysis of different types of barriers and perceptions patterns emerged that described the categories of pessimistic and optimistic regarding leadership career momentum. The highest view referenced was hopeful and optimistic. Pessimistic was greater than expanded vision, which explains the analysis of the researcher that female Christian ministry leaders are utilizing coping mechanisms to face barriers.

Table 7

Codes for Leadership Career Momentum

Key Words and Phrases	Initial Category	Example from Transcript Including Source	Initial Themes
Vision	View of Female Leader	I had a vision that leadership loved but it was not acknowledged right away. (Participant 1)	Leadership Carrier Momentum
Optimistic	View of Female Leader	We have to keep moving forward even if they are trying to hinder and hurt. (Participant 3)	Leadership Carrier Momentum

Pessimistic	View of Female Leader	I do not want to be bothered anymore. (Participant 10)	Leadership Carrier Momentum
Hopeful	View of Female Leader	I begin to relate it to a prior bad experience but I was hopeful	Leadership Carrier Momentum

The fifth theme that emerged from the researcher was how the female Christian ministry leaders were able to cope with the internal, external barriers previously observed, and hand coded. The researcher previously identified that one way was by the female Christian ministry leader's perception. A deeper observation made by the researcher was that changing the perception of the female Christian ministry leader became a way of dealing with barriers. As the researcher continued to analyze frequently used words such as collaboration, relaxation, prayer, and mentorship, training, development, counseling, meditation, and regroup were observed and hand coded. The analysis by the researcher identified patterns of the frequently used words that revealed two categories, which were coping mechanisms and not coping well. Out of the 10 participants, the researcher observed that some participants were not coping well. The frequently used hand coded words that were analyzed for the category of not coping well were weighted down, altered, and wounded. The theme coping mechanisms emerged from the two categories. However, the participants that have sustained the third theme, which is internal and external barriers, are observed by the researcher, as the female Christian ministry leaders that are not coping well.

Table 8

Codes for Coping Mechanisms

Key Words and Phrases	Initial Category	Example from Transcript Including Source	Initial Themes
Regroup	Dealing with barriers	I have to regroup sometimes. (Participant 3)	Coping Mechanism
Collaboration	Dealing with barriers	The collaborative relations work hand in hand. (Participant 3)	Coping Mechanism
Counseling	Dealing with barriers	There is safety in the multitude of counsel. (Participant)	Coping Mechanism

Mediation	Dealing with barriers	Meditation and quiet time is crucial.(Participant 4)	Coping Mechanism
Mentorship	Dealing with barriers	I was mentored by older women that trained me. (Participant 2)	Coping Mechanism
Training/Development	Dealing with barriers	I believe that training, mentorship and development going into Christian leadership is important. (Participant 4)	Coping Mechanism
Prayer	Dealing with barriers	Prayer and just talking to God. (Prayer 2)	Coping Mechanism
Rest	Dealing with barriers	Then we rest, retreat, and get ready to fight again. (Participant 3)	Coping Mechanism
Relaxation	Dealing with barriers	Relaxation by going to conferences. (Participant 3)	Coping Mechanism

One important concept of the case study is triangulation. Stake (2005) defines it as "a process of using multiple perceptions to clarify meaning, verifying the repeatability of an observation or interpretation." (p. 454). This source is essential to elude misconception. In addition, triangulation can be achieved through repetitiveness of data gathered and routine challenges to explanations. Various steps within the triangulation process are conducive to conducting a qualitative case study. The researcher formulated triangulation of interviews, journal field notes, and questionnaires to properly interpret and code the data. Grouping the consistent and relevant experiences from interviews, questionnaires, and journal field notes established core themes. A final review of the identified, relevant, and consistent themes was compared to the transcriptions to ensure the themes were unambiguous and appropriate. All categories, themes, and codes from each participant were validated by triangulation of interviews, questionnaires, and journal field notes, and then structured into transcribed descriptions of the experiences. The verbal elements that described the experiences articulated by the participants were collected to form a characterized description of the experience. Both verbal elements and characterized descriptions of the meaning and substance of the experiences were incorporated with the identified themes, which formed multiple descriptions of the experience.

First, the researcher identified the theory concerning the topic. Secondly, a specific and unique phenomenon was identified, which aids in the selection of research questions. After the research questions were developed, the researcher collected the data from interviews, questionnaires, and journal field notes. The following steps were to organize the data by hand coding the common relevant words and phrases, and then developing patterns that clustered into categories and themes related to the topic.

Interviews, questionnaires, and journal field notes were transcribed, coded, and themed to answer the research questions below. The five common themes were: (a) Female Perception of Leadership (b) Characteristics of Female Leadership (c) Internal and External Barriers (d) Leadership Momentum (e) Coping Mechanisms. Specifically, each research question below was answered via the stated data collection instruments:

R1: How do women in leadership identify and perceive internal and external barriers in Christian ministry leadership attainment? (Information from questionnaires audio-taped open-ended interviews and notes (Stake, 1978, 1995, 1998; Yin, 2009). The interview question and questionnaire, along with sub questions that linked the data as internal barriers and learned behaviors are listed below:

R2: What steps have women in leadership positions taken to overcome barriers in Christian ministry? (Information from questionnaires, audio-taped open-ended interviews and notes (Stake, 1978, 1995, 1998; Yin, 2009). The interview question and questionnaire, along with sub questions that correlate the data as external barriers and inherent characteristics are listed below:

R3: Why do women in Christian leadership positions persevere in their commitment to serve despite obstacles when considering their own inherent and learned characteristics for leadership and how do they define those characteristics? (Information from questionnaires, audio-taped open-ended interviews and notes (Stake, 1978, 1995, 1998; Yin, 2009). The interview question and questionnaire, along with sub questions that correlate the data as personal barriers and female perceptions are listed below:

R4: What personal, social, and perceptual barriers do women face when they seek Christian leadership positions? (Information from questionnaires, audio-taped open-ended interviews and notes (Stake, 1978, 1995, 1998; Yin, 2009). The interview question and questionnaire, along with sub questions that correlate the data as Characteristics of leadership, Coping Mechanisms, and Career Momentum are listed below:

Results

The participants all began with a detailed description of their experience as a woman in ministry. Each expression from participants using triangulation from interviews, questionnaires, and journal field notes relevant to the experience was listed. Each statement was extrapolated to ensure that the expression was relevant to the experience. Expressions not related to the experience were placed in a special category called interesting quotes. One important concept of the case study is triangulation. Stake (2005) defines it as "a process of using multiple perceptions to clarify meaning, verifying the repeatability of an observation or interpretation." (p. 454). This source was essential to elude misconception. In addition, triangulation can be achieved through repetitiveness of data gathered and routine challenges to explanation.

All interviews, questionnaires, and journal field notes revealed dedication and commitment with years of service in Christian ministry. Five common themes resulted throughout the questionnaire, interview, and field notes. The common themes extrapolated included: (a) Female Perception of Leadership (b) Characteristics of Female Leadership (c) Internal and External Barriers (d) Leadership Momentum (e) Coping Mechanisms. The journal field notes recorded the effects of the role that barriers played in attitude, behavior, and disposition of the participants. The participants' gestures, body language, voice tones, and emotions all validated the five common themes.

The researcher noted in the journal field notes that 4 out of 10 participants found it hard to discuss their experiences, and often had to look away or not able to make direct eye contact with the researcher, while expressing that there were internal barriers that still needed to be dealt with. The defensive and hurt emotions of participants' experiences identified that internal and external barriers do exist. However, 6 out of 10 had a desire to dig deep to identify the root of their experiences as coping mechanisms were discussed. The researcher noted in the journal field notes of sighs of relief and instead of the participant looking down; the head movement looked up toward the ceiling as if there may be hope. The researcher noted in the journal field notes of how some participant's voice tones gave a sensation of concern regarding the current times and increased in intensity regarding the future for women in leadership.

The researcher noted that 9 out of 10 participants became seemingly stronger in voice tone and disposition as the interviews concluded. This demonstrates perseverance, motivation, inspiration, and a sense of determination. Some participants even gave the researcher a high-five as they exclaimed, "I got this or I can do this." However, also noted there was one participant that expresses the desire not to move forward as a leader, while looking down at the floor. Additionally, 2 out of 10 participants took the time to think long and hard before answering the questions, because they were not exactly sure where they stood regarding their perceptions of leadership. The researcher noted that body language and gestures such as frowns, shaking of heads in disdain, the rolling of eyes, crying, and anger demonstrated offense, insecurity, intimidation, fear, and uncertainty as perceptions were discussed.

The intensity of some participant's voice became rocky when describing their perception of leadership that included bias, judgement, and discrimination. The researcher noted that while discussing career momentum tears were shed as participants expressed feelings of entrapment and facial expressions of confusion trying to figure out why female Christian ministry leaders have to encounter such disgrace and misfortune. The interviews were captured on NVIVO, which extrapolated codes, common themes, words, and phrases from multiple sources, such as the interview, questionnaire, and field notes. Below are the descriptive codes and thematic ideas that emerged from this process. Figure 3 is an illustration of the five themes that emerged from the coded data and an explanation is included in the following text.

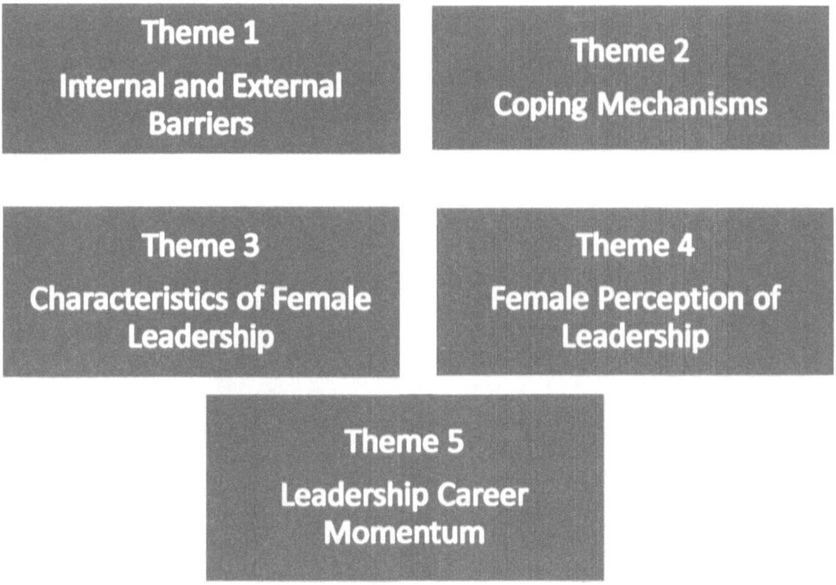

Theme 1 Internal and External Barriers	**Theme 2** Coping Mechanisms
Theme 3 Characteristics of Female Leadership	**Theme 4** Female Perception of Leadership

Theme 5
Leadership Career Momentum

Figure 3. Common themes that emerged from the coded data.

Internal barriers vs. external barriers. During the interviews and questionnaire process, participants were asked about barriers that women face as a leader in Christian ministry, 100%, or 10 out of 10 women consistently mentioned was the struggle of internal and external barriers. Additionally, the participants described internal barriers as having to deal with internal challenges from within. Some internal barriers identified are intimidation, insecurity, and fear, and rejection, defeat, discouraged, belittled, weary, and forsaken. The participants described external barriers as things that seemingly are beyond self-control. External barriers were voiced as disadvantaged, disapproval, unaccepted by male and female individuals or groups. Participant 1 spoke of external barriers in terms of intimidation:

> I have barriers from other women in ministry, intimidation. If I have a new idea, they are hesitant to support me because it was not their idea. From men in the ministry, they are hesitant to support me because they feel intimidated because it sheds more light on the female verses the male. Tradition has taught us that man is first and it is often carried over in the aspect of ideas and concepts that as a woman in leadership you have to get permission if you want to administer or minister to others in Christian ministry. Especially if you are coming into a new place of ministry, where the headship may know of

me but the members that are both female and male are slow to embrace, receive, and come together. Nevertheless, it is all rooted in intimidation.

Other participants spoke of external barriers in terms of rituals, leadership, male influence, insecurities, and opposition. For instance, Participant 2 spoke of barriers as issues with those in authority who have set traditional protocols that restrain female Christian ministry leaders from serving people in need.

> The barriers I have faced are with those in authority who want to be acknowledged for the things that God has given you to do. It is emotional when your mind is following the instructions of God and ministry to the people but you have to remember the order of tradition and protocol. There are so many rituals, traditions, and obligations that you have to consider prior to obeying what God want you to do. It is hurtful that when you do obey you are reprimanded for not obeying man. (Participant 2)

Participant 3 spoke of barriers as waiting on the approval of male leadership and female Christian ministry leaders cannot allow themselves to be hindered.

> I had a vision that leadership loved but it was not acknowledged right away. It appeared to have been ignored until finally the leadership found time to review what I had submitted. I felt like it was a barrier because I was waiting on him to approve it but he never did. However, as I continued to move forward anyway the male leader finally came around. We hinder ourselves because we are waiting on an approval from a man. (Participant 3)

Participant 4 spoke of barriers as difficulty separating her personal relationship with God while having a dislike for the way things are done in Church.

> I struggle with separating my relationship and my love for God and my dislike for the church and how I feel about God and how I feel about the Church. Wanting to be obedient to God but dealing with the

> realm of the church. I am not pleased with what I see with the church and how we operate how we represent God in the world. Trying to find mentors and other women that you can find wisdom from that are not trying to clone you into them, they are not intimidated, or they are not trying to kill you. Barriers are encountered with the men of the church. (Participant 4)

Participant 5 spoke of barriers as the ability for female Christian ministry leaders to remain focused and steadfast regardless of what they may come confront.

> God has to cut away things in our lives and in the lives of others. Although we may face barriers, we have to remain focused so that we can continue to be circumcised to God's liking. Even when we are hurt, disappointed, and feel rejected we must remain steadfast and in position. Move when God gives us clearance. (Participant 5)

Participant 6 spoke about not allowing anything to deter female Christian ministry leaders from doing what God has instructed them to do.

> When God gives you something to do, you move on it regardless. When you present it and do not receive approval, you keep moving on it. Whether they think God gave it to you or not you still follow through with it and allow God to deal with the others. Do not every allow another person or group to stop you from doing what He has called you to do. You stay faithful to God and stay in the word of God. (Participant 6)

Participant 7 spoke about the struggles that female Christian ministry leaders face as barriers prior to even facing other people.

> It makes me angry sometimes and I constantly have to remind myself of the bigger picture. I have to stay focused even as I am dealing with my own struggles doubting myself and feeling belittled. (Participant 7)

Participant 8 speaks about insecurities that exist for female Christian ministry leaders, but they must continue to serve with external barriers present.

> I am being stretched out of my comfort zone because it is forcing me to be out front when I would just like to be unnoticed. I deal with my own self-insecurities prior to even meeting face to face with those that are imposed upon me from external sources. (Participant 8)

Participant 9 speaks about the barriers of expectations of herself and the expectations that are present from others as a female Christian ministry leader.

> My largest barrier would be expectancy; expectancy of myself and the expectations from others. So many people expect so many different things from me. I am expected to do everything right. It makes me feel like I have not been walking in what God wanted me to do. I will not do any more facades or portray anything other than who God has called me to be. I

> expect to do the will of God. Whoever understands or do not understand. It is my expectation to walk into what I am called to do. (Participant 9)

Participant 10 speaks about the barriers of insecurity of female Christian ministry leaders and the superiority imposed by men.

> Men see themselves superior and to be a women preaching and teaching in the pulpit. You have to deal with insecurities from them and you are not called according to their expectations. Even if you do implement what God is calling you to do they have a problem with you, because you being a woman. They are upset because you can actually hear from God. Men are intimidated because it is something that is not traditionally accepted. A subtle action is taken toward you because you are a woman. You have to say things a certain way. You have to sit in certain seats, etc. It makes me feel less than even though you know that you are not but after coming against it so

long you start succumb to it or submit to you or you digress. I overcome because I realize that it seems to be common and I understand that I am not the only one dealing with it. (Participant 10)

Internal and external barriers. Participant 1 speaks about social barriers that women face as a leader in Christian ministry. She identifies social barriers as not having acceptance, approval, or support from males and some females that are leadership, which has become a tradition.

> Traditional barriers are a part of society. The societal barriers are set up and created within the church. The barriers can be several things. I have barriers from other women in ministry, intimidation. If I have a new idea, they are hesitant to support me because it was not their idea. From men in the ministry, they are hesitant to support me because they feel intimidated because it sheds more light on the female verses the male. Tradition has taught us that man is first and it is often carried over in the aspect of ideas and

> concepts that as a woman in leadership you have to get permission if you want to administer or minister to others in Christian ministry. Especially if you are coming into a new place of ministry, where the headship may know of me but the members that are both female and male are slow to embrace, receive, and come together. (Participant 1)

Participant 2 spoke about how societal barriers have an effect on the total being of a female in Christian ministry as a leader and how heavy it can weight on the emotions.

> Nevertheless, it is all rooted in intimidation. It makes me take a step back because it affected me emotionally, psychologically, spiritually, and physically. It made me think I should slow down the process of what it is that I desire to put in motion, but I have never struggled with the fact that I know what I was created to do. It became an emotional weight. I felt weighted down emotionally. I became sad inside because I begin to relate it to a prior bad

> experience but I was hopeful. It was psychologically challenging because the bad experiences kept replaying in my mind. (Participant 2)

Participant 4 spoke about the barriers as a comparison of confidence in the professional workplace verses the lack of confidence in ministry.

> My confidence level is very high there. I feel safe and secure verses how it is translated into what I do in ministry. I think the same skills should be easily translated. Maybe because I felt better equipped in the corporate world because I have a degree or I have certain experience there, but I now understand that my whole life experience has been equipping me as a women leader for ministry. It took me some time to realize how to build that same level of confidence, but it has been an enlightening journey understanding that I am in God. I finally do not feel like I have to come from a certain pedigree or background or take a certain traditional path to get

there. However, I am here simply because God called me I am already equipped and justified to be in this place and keeping my own voice as a female leader and not feeling like I had to ascribe to a certain voice. (Participant 4)

Noted in Figure 4 are the topics of discussion mentioned both during interview and in questionnaire were identified internal and external barriers that are quite challenging as a female Christian ministry leader. Participants noted constant opposition, a desire to quit and give up, disobey God, and sit in the background. However, participants also perceive the need to keep moving forward in spite of those barriers because obeying God is priority. Theme 1 correlates and answers RQ1 listed below.

The chart below is a breakdown of the additional topics that were expressed during the interview and questionnaire. Out of 10 participants, 3 or 30% of the participants would rather sit in the background than to be a female Christian ministry leader. Two out of 10 or 20% of the participants have struggled and continue to struggle with disobeying God because of barriers. 2 out of 10 or 20% consider quitting and giving up as the best option. 3 out of 10 or 30% of the participants despise having to face continual opposition.

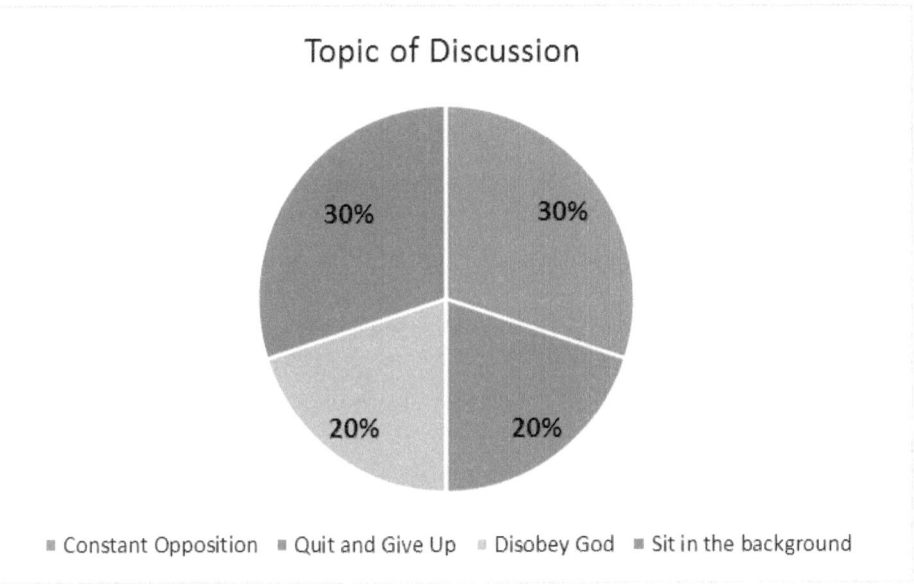

Figure 4. Topics of discussion relevant to internal and external barriers.

Sixty percent or 6 out of 10 participants voiced with great concern the need for coping mechanisms for current female Christian ministry leaders and the generations to follow. Additionally, expressed by a participant during the interviews was the need for female Christian ministry leaders to routinely take advantage of just being a person and allow the leader role to retreat when necessary.

Participant 3 speaks about how it initially effects the female Christian ministry leader and that relaxation can help you regain focus.

> It initially makes me want to quit and give up. I then get that second wind after revamping and understanding that I am only human. It reminds me of a war and how there are times we fight small battles within the war. However, it also helps me to understand the importance of rest, retreat, and get ready to fight again. (Participant 3)

Table 9 includes the coping mechanisms according to hierarchy, and are ranked by the level of importance per participant. The participants concluded that collaboration was the most important coping mechanism, because it allows for individuals, groups to adapt, and finding common ground. Relaxation was ranked the same as collaboration by the participants because of a desired relaxed environment to be able to serve others effectively and relaxation in regards to restoring one's self in an effort to continue in service. The next hierarchical coping mechanism is prayer. Prayer was ranked the third most important mechanism during the interview process. Closely after prayer was rest. Rest was ranked the same as mentorship. The participants expressed the need to rest mentally, physically, and emotionally from the responsibility of leadership at times. The participants expressed that mentorship is lacking for the female Christian ministry leader and having a mentor would increase the ability for women to cope with barriers faced. Meditation, counseling, and regroup were all ranked the same by the participants.

Participant 1 spoke about counseling as a way of coping with the challenges of being a female Christian ministry leader.

> Wise counsel. Finding a counselor that can help me is important to my success. There is safety in the multitude of counsel. God has more than one way to get things accomplished. I seek the soundness of others that are outside of the four walls of the church. God's people are everywhere. We have to be open to listen and discern God in every aspect imaginable. I think it is crucial to develop relationship with God so you can hear His voice and His directions. (Participant 1)

Participant 2 speaks about the importance of prayer and communing with God through conversation at any time.

> Prayer and just talking to God. Having a conversation with God is important. You do not have to be all loud or deep but just having a conversation with God throughout the day or while you are driving in your car. Pray with expectations and knowing that God can handle any situation. Pray for God to bless

you also, regardless of the barriers that are being faced. (Participant 2)

Participant 3 spoke about doing various recreational activities to cope with the barriers that female Christian ministry leaders face.

Rest, relaxation, regroup, and recalibrate. Going to a conference to meet other female leaders and participate in collaborative conversation or take a trip to a place that you have never been. Try going to musically stimulating events such as the symphony, theater, ballet, or the opera. Introduce yourself to different types of things that will allow you to engage with self and the human needs of yourself." It initially makes me want to quit. I then get that second wind after revamping. It reminds me of a war and how there are times we fight small battles within the war. Then we rest, retreat, and get ready to fight again. (Participant 3)

Participant 4 spoke about translating thoughts on paper as a way of coping with barriers and being disciplined to hear God during the storms.

> Reading books on specific topics and journaling your thoughts, ideas, and concepts can eliminate areas of frustration. I believe, sometimes we have to realize there is more to us than Christian ministry, as we may know it. There is a whole world out there that we need to embrace absent the human imposed barriers. Being disciplined enough to have the meditation and quiet time is crucial to listening to God's thoughts concerning us. (Participant 4)

Participant 9 spoke about taking a self-assessment and dealing with self as a coping mechanism for the barriers that female Christian ministry leaders face.

> I cope by dealing with me. I address the root of why I feel the way I do as a result to what is being done or said. It pushed me out of the box and made me

accept who I am and alter as need be to fortify for what I may be encountering.

Participant 9 went on to say:

> I stopped and retreated because people expect you to be consistent and committed no matter what, but they will not be accountable themselves. I looked around and realized I did not know whom I was anymore and dealing with that was frightening. I lost my effectiveness because I was so drained from trying to meet everyone else's needs and change according to what they wanted. I had to start coping with who I was and rebuild myself to do what He is calling to do. You have to keep pushing in-spite of the encounter. (Participant 9)

Sixty percent of the participants have identified coping mechanisms and ways to overcome barriers in Christian ministry. However, it has been a challenge for many to find ways to overcome and some have even stopped leading.

Participant 10 spoke about how female Christian ministry leaders should expect barriers because God never said things would be easy.

> I often think of Jonah because he did not want to go because the people will not listen or receive. The reality is that people will try to stop and block you. However, we are held accountable for thing that is irrevocable. We are still responsible for doing what He called us to do. We assume that because God gave it to us that we will not encounter barriers, but we will. (Participant 10)

Coping mechanisms. Participant 1 spoke about the cultural barrier as being religion, how it can place a wedge between God and the female Christian ministry leaders.

> It made me discouraged in the sense of being tired of the opposition and having to fight against so many challenges. I am vexed at times. I wanted to take a back seat and only move when I felt like it not has God needed me to do. I did not want to be responsible

for what God told me. God and I started not agreeing with each other because I wanted to be left alone. I am sick of the religious type of leadership instead of the ministry aspect. I know that I am called but that is different from doing what you are called to do. (Participant 1)

Participant 2 spoke about being obedient to cultural barriers comes as a priority before obeying God.

The barriers I have faced are with those in authority who want to be acknowledged for the things that God has given you to do. It is emotional when your mind is following the instructions of God and ministry to the people but you have to remember the order of tradition and protocol. There are so many rituals, traditions, and obligations that you have to consider, prior to obeying what God wants you to do. It is hurtful that when you do obey you are reprimanded for not obeying man. I often feel emotionally, psychologically, and spiritually torn and hurt between what God directs me to do, and what man desires for me to do. I also feel torn because even when you follow what tradition and man wants you to do they will change in the midst just to trick you up or make you look bad. I feel hesitant, reluctant, and cautious. Other leadership becomes intimidated because they are not acknowledged. (Participant 2)

Participant 3 spoke about how female Christian ministry leaders are ignored because of cultural barriers and often times never receive approval from male leadership.

It appeared to have been ignored until finally the leadership found time to review what I had submitted. God was telling me to get it done prior to a certain time but I was waiting on approval from male leadership. I have learned that when you obey God everything will fall into place. I felt like it was a barrier because I was waiting on him to approve it but he never did. However, as I continued to move forward anyway the male leader finally came around.

I learned that the barrier was good because it was not for that particular location because it would have put limitations on it. We hinder ourselves because we are waiting on an approval from a man. It is a war physically, emotionally, and spiritually with others and us. I was my own physical barrier because I chose to wait for approval instead of moving according to the instructions that God had given me. God sent confirmation repeatedly but we decide to struggle with the approval of man, which blocks us from doing what we are supposed to do. Our physical flesh is our greatest barrier. We have to keep moving forward regardless even if they are trying to hinder and hurt us in one regard we have to keep moving. (Participant 3)

Participant 4 spoke about the cultural barrier of risking a personal relationship with God for the sake of pleasing the Church.

I experience traditional barriers and lack of wisdom and my disdain for the church. I struggle with separating my relationship and my love for God and my dislike for the church and how I feel about God and how I feel about the Church. Wanting to be obedient to God but dealing with the realm of the church. I am not pleased with what I see with the church and how we operate how we represent God in the world. Trying to find mentors and other women that you can find wisdom from that are not trying to clone you into them, they are not intimidated, or they are not trying to kill you. Barriers are with the men of the church. (Participant 4)

Table 9

Coping Mechanisms Frequently Mentioned

Coping Mechanism	Number of Frequency (Participant)
Collaboration	10
Relaxation	10
Prayer	8

Mentorship	6
Rest	6
Training and Development	5
Counseling	2
Meditation	2
Regroup	2

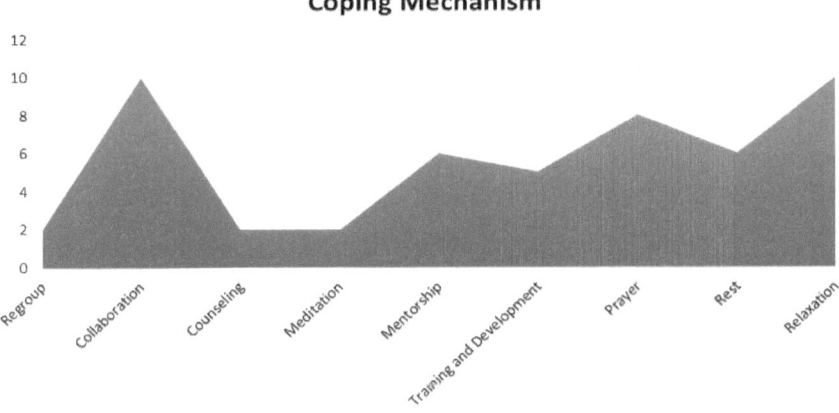

Figure 5. Coping mechanism hierarchies as grouped by hierarchy.

Thirty percent or 3 out of 10 participants are not coping well. The 3 participants have stopped moving forward as a female Christian ministry leader, need time to heal because of wounds, or have changed to fit the approval of others. Participant 8 the lack of motivation and feeling alone as a female Christian ministry leader.

> I felt weighted down emotionally. I became sad inside because I begin to relate it to a prior bad experience but I was hopeful. It was psychologically challenging because the bad experiences kept replaying in my mind. God and I started not agreeing with each other because I wanted to be left alone. I am sick of the religious type of leadership instead of the ministry aspect. My help was not accepted or was recommended that it be altered in order to be able to implement my vision. I have a barrier of motivating people to just be apart or take advantage of the benefits that I am providing. I experience no support from other women. I have to keep encouraging myself because I would rather sit in the back and support others instead of being out in front. (Participant 8)

Participant 9 added some informative discussion on how others' needs resulted in why she stopped her work as a leader:

> I stopped because people expect you to be consistent and committed but they will not be accountable themselves. I looked around and realized I did not know whom I was anymore. I lost my effectiveness because I was so drained from everyone else's needs. I had to start coping with who I was and rebuild myself to do what He is calling to do. You have to keep pushing in-spite of the encounter. Feelings of being unappreciated were evident.

Table 10

Coping Mechanisms

Theme 2	Number of Participants
Coping Mechanisms	6
Response not received participants admit to not coping well.	3
Outlier	1

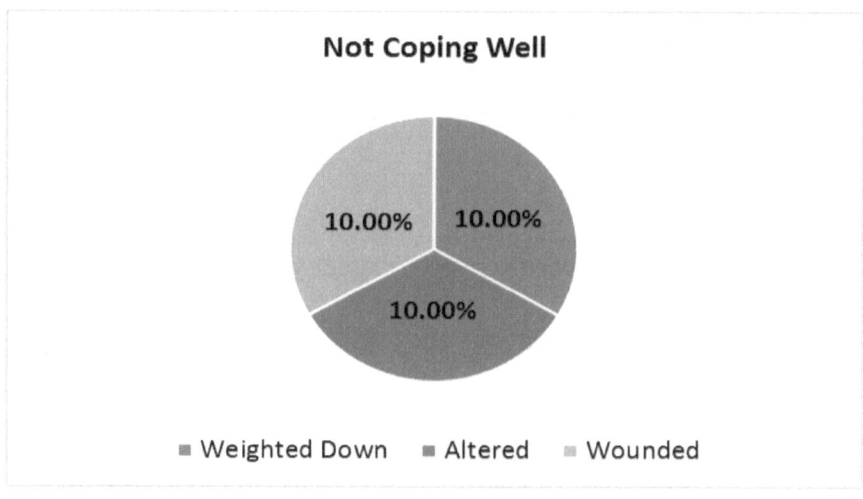

Figure 6. Breakdown of theme related to not coping well.

One hundred percent or 10 out of 10 participants conveyed a positive view regarding the characteristics of being a female leader. The inherent characteristics listed below have taught the participants how to forge forward in spite of the barriers faced. Fifty percent of the participants have revamped, recalibrated, and reevaluated the ways of how things are done, and the expectations they have of themselves by learning how to let go, rechanneled my focus, adjust expectations, and follow through with leadership assignment. Characteristics of female leaders are defined as motivated, unstoppable, determined, relentless, fearless, and strengthened.

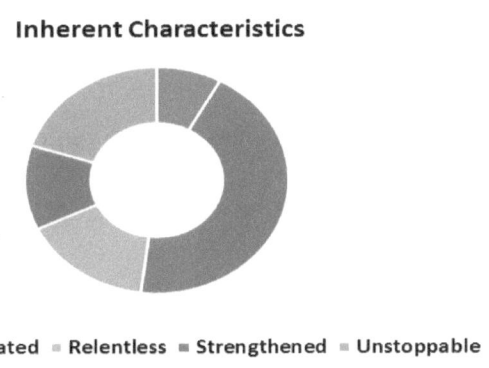

Figure 7. Participants' identified inherent characteristics that are attributes of success.

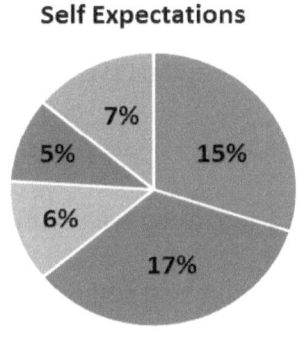

Figure 8. Participants' explanations of self-expectations.

Participant 1 spoke about refocusing on the big picture instead of man-made expectations for female Christian ministry leaders.

It has been positive and rewarding because I know this is what I have been created to do. It made me discouraged in the sense of being tired of the opposition and having to fight against so many challenges. I am vexed at times. I wanted to take a back seat and only move when I felt like it not has God needed me to do. I did not want to be responsible for what God told me. God and I started not agreeing with each other because I wanted to be left alone. I am sick of the religious type of leadership instead of the ministry aspect. I know that I am called but that is different from doing what you are called to do. He gives me scripture and songs to make me determined to keep pressing. He rechanneled my focus for why I am doing what He called me to do. It is not about man but about doing what God needs of you. It is very disheartening when you are trying to catch up from past errors or missed decisions. I get weary and tired. My soul gets tired and weary, not my flesh. (Participant 1)

Participant 2 spoke about having a good experience and that barriers have propelled her as a female Christian ministry leader, to move forward in spite of opposition.

I get fearless and unstoppable because I remember the things that God has brought me through before and it helps me to fortify for what is coming and what will be next. It pushes me to pray more to seek God more and see what God is going to do next. It pushes me to do better. When opposition comes, it causes me to become relentless and want to overcome the obstacle. When I feel like the opposition is trying to tear me down or belittle me by attempting to step on me and keep me down it strengthens me to fight. My overall experience is good. Because I am, mature and seasoned because I was mentored by older women that trained me. (Participant 2)

Participant 3 went on to say:

It has been good, it has been enlightening, and I am still learning. I want to give up until I refocus and refuse not to do my part as a soldier that is on the battlefield in the war. (Participant 3)

Participant 4 spoke about not being defeated as a female Christian ministry leader and moves forward with determination.

I am motivated and fearless because the opposition should have killed me when he had the chance because I am moving forward regardless. This journey has been a very long learning experience through the tears, friction, and rejection that comes with being a Christian Ministry leader, as a woman because now I know just how much God loves me, and just how much I have to offer someone else. (Participant 4)

Participant 5 spoke about having a different view regarding her life as a female Christian ministry leader.

> I use to look at being a woman leader in Christian ministry as a negative thing, but I am now changing my outlook to view it more of a positive aspect. (Participant 5)

Participant 6 spoke about the pros and cons of being a female Christian ministry leader and is motivated with a positive outlook.

> My overall experience is positive because the good outweighs the bad. It motivates me to keep going in spite of the obstacles that I may face. There are days that I have to encourage myself, but I know that God is counting on me. (Participant 6)

Participant 7 spoke about properly dealing with the barriers as a female Christian ministry leader and experience brings about knowledge.

> I would say that my experience is both positive and negative. I am moving forward, but I have not totally

> learned how to properly deal with some of the barriers that I face. I believe as I have more experiences, then I will become more knowledgeable on how to handle different situations that are presented. (Participant 7)

Participant 8 spoke about having a positive experience and the bad experiences propelled her forward.

> I would say that my experience would be positive. Even with the negative things or what I felt was bad really was working for my good especially for where I am now in leadership. I am motivated to keep going because I see how God is keeping me. I am determined not to let Him down, because He has never failed me. (Participant 8)

Participant 9 spoke about her overall experience as being positive and having a more intimate relationship with God.

> My overall experience has been positive because it is bringing me closer to God and becoming more dedicated to Him. I was affected because I just stop

> wasting time in areas that were not productive. When only two or three would show up, I would just call it quits and stop sacrificing for lack of support. However, I have come to realize that this is greater than I am. I am relentless and unstoppable. (Participant 9)

Participant 10 spoke about how as a female Christian ministry leader she needed to be healed.

> I am currently facing myself in the mirror because I do not want to be bothered anymore. I have not seen the benefits of the sacrifice of taking on the barriers that are presented. Internal barriers exist because I am in need of repair from the things that have happened externally. My mind, spirit, and emotions need to be repaired. I will not move forward until I know God has reestablished me. (Participant 10)

Characteristics of female leadership. Participant 1 spoke about the characteristics of being a female leader as steadfast.

> Although we may face barriers, we have to remain focused so that we can continue to be circumcised to God's liking. Even when we are hurt, disappointed, and feel rejected we must remain steadfast and in position. Move when God gives us clearance. (Participant 1)

Participant 2 spoke about following the required traditions of man, but female Christian ministry leaders must keep moving in what God told you to do.

> When God gives you something to do, you move on it regardless. When you present it and do not receive approval, you keep moving on it. Whether they think God gave it to you or not you still follow through with it and allow God to deal with the others. Do not every allow another person or group to stop you from doing what He has called you to do. You stay faithful to God and stay in the word of God. (Participant 2)

Participant 2 also spoke about assumptions of barriers, and the expectations of female Christian ministry leaders.

> The reality is that people will try to stop and block you. However, we are held accountable for thing that is irrevocable. We are still responsible for doing what He called us to do. We assume that because God gave it to us that we will not encounter barriers, but we will. (Participant 2)

Table 11 demonstrates the number of participants that function and operate in the characteristics of a leader specifically the characteristics also expected of a woman in leadership, which are noted on the left side of Figure 9. The characteristics of a female leader in Christian ministry can be expanded according to the participants by the barriers that are constantly faced. These characteristics are called inherent characteristics, which are noted on the right side of Figure 9.

Table 11

Inherent and Learned Characteristics

Theme 3	Number of Participants
Characteristics of Female Leadership	10
Inherent Characteristics	5

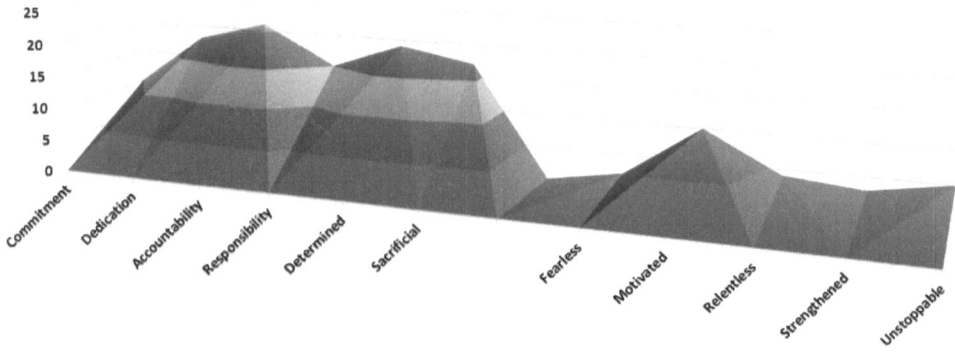

Figure 9. Comparison of participants' leader and inherent characteristics.

Eighty percent or 8 out of 10 participants expressed a perception of disdain for leadership. Therefore, perceptual, social, and personal barriers were articulated during the interviews. The participants voiced a need to place blame on others and self because of being seemingly forced to accept or adopt routines, rituals, and traditions that constrain the participant from leading effectively. Additionally, the participant's perceptions are stained by emotional, physical, psychological, and spiritual barriers. As a result, participants have admitted to holding resentments against male leadership and have caused self-sabotage by not yielding to directives given.

Participant 1 spoke of digressing and halting the process due to the effects of barriers as a female Christian ministry leader.

> I have not second-guessed myself or doubted who I am. However, it makes me take a step back because it affected me emotionally, psychologically, spiritually, and physically. It made me think I should slow down the process of what it is that I desire to put in motion, but I have never struggled with the fact that I know what I was created to do. It became an emotional weight. I felt weighted down emotionally. I became sad inside because I begin to relate it to a prior bad experience but I was hopeful. It was psychologically challenging because the bad

> experiences kept replaying in my mind. (Participant 1)

Participant 2 spoke about the struggle that is faced as a female Christian ministry leader between tradition and God.

> I often feel emotionally, psychologically, and spiritually torn and hurt between what God directs me to do, and what man desires for me to do. I also feel torn because even when you follow what tradition and man wants you to do they will change in the midst just to trick you up or make you look bad. I feel hesitant, reluctant, and cautious. (Participant 2)

Participant 3 spoke about following God's instructions regardless of what hindrances female Christian ministry leaders face.

> It is a war physically, emotionally, and spiritually with others and ourselves. I was my own physical barrier because I chose to wait for approval instead of moving according to the instructions that God had

> given me. God sent confirmation repeatedly but we decide to struggle with the approval of man, which blocks us from doing what we are supposed to do. Our physical flesh is our greatest barrier. We have to keep moving forward regardless even if they are trying to hinder and hurt us in one regard we have to keep moving. (Participant 3)

Participant 4 spoke about the different feelings she experiences as a professional female leader and a Christian ministry leader.

> I did not realize the emotional, psychological, and spiritual struggles I would encounter when we (my husband and I) started the ministry that as my husband and I equally doing things professionally together is different in ministry. Women or wives are not considered equal in ministry but are held just as accountable. Men do not want women to speak or say anything. As a woman, I am trying to be better in ministry but better may not what most ministries or

men desire for women. There is an inconsistency and my struggle is with being who God has called me to be and who man tries to force me to be. (Participant 4)

Participant 5 spoke about being the barrier that she faces as a female Christian ministry leader.

I have been my own barrier because of my struggles internally. I often wonder why God chose me because I did not choose to be the women in leadership. I prefer to be in the background and at home alone. I wonder why God chose me when He knows what I would rather be doing. I am struggling with embracing where God has me. I have jumped out of the box this year but I am still looking back to see if the box is still there. I still question if I am good enough. (Participant 5)

Participant 7 spoke about a being disrespected in a working environment where a population of men are greater than women.

> I feel like my issues are within myself and with others because I work in a male dominated field. Working with a staff that are older than I am and do not provide a certain level of respect. As a woman I am questioned when I give directives even though I am a leader. They have to check with the men before they accept my directives. I am affected internally where I question my ability. I constantly have to tell myself that I have the ability to do this. (Participant 7)

Participant 8 spoke about the lack of support from leadership as a female Christian ministry leader.

> I struggle with tradition and approval. I was given so many things to do from God but my leaders did not appreciate it or were not in support of it because of how society would perceive it. My help was not accepted or was recommended that it be altered in order to be able to implement my vision. I have a barrier of motivating people to just be apart or take

> advantage of the benefits that I am providing. I experience no support from other women. I have to keep encouraging myself because I would rather sit in the back and support others instead of being out in front. (Participant 8)

Women have and are still in leadership positions and younger generations are currently seeking leadership positions in Christian ministry within nonprofit organizations. Nevertheless, being a female Christian ministry leader presents various types of barriers that are not always voiced or considered. Eighty percent of the participants interviewed perceive that women seeking Christian leadership positions will face personal, social, and perceptual barriers.

Female perception of leadership. Participant 1 spoke about the baggage that barriers create when experienced by a female Christian ministry leader.

> I blame it on culture, society, and traditional baggage. We carry around so much baggage. We can

> do all the right things and still will encounter challenges and opposition because it is the will of God. He is going to allow things to happen to help us. (Participant 1)

Participant 2 spoke about the increase of knowledge from the barriers experienced.

> This journey has been a very learning experience through the tears, friction, and rejection that comes with being a Christian Ministry leader, as a woman because now I know just how much God loves me, and just how much I have to offer someone else. (Participant 2)

Participant 4 spoke about the inequality between male and female with the standards of accountability.

> I did not realize the emotional, psychological, and spiritual struggles I would encounter when we (my husband and I) started the ministry that as my husband and I equally doing things professionally together is different in ministry. Women or wives are

not considered equal in ministry but are held just as accountable. Men do not want women to speak or say anything. As a woman, I am trying to be better in ministry but better is not what most ministries or men desire for women. There is an inconsistency and my struggle is with being who God has called me to be and who man tries to force me to be. (Participant 3)

I was angry and wanted to revert. I wanted to revert to what was familiar in the world and I felt tricked. I am not a punk anymore and I do not have the option to quick. I spiritually wanted to just stop and not do anything ever again. I was not able to trace God or hear Him. I wanted to stop and at certain points, I needed to stop. I survived. (Participant 4)

Participant 5 said that, "I use to look at being a woman leader in Christian ministry as a negative thing but I am now changing my outlook to view it more of a positive aspect."

Participant 6 had a more overall positive experience. She said, "My overall experience would be positive. Even with the negative things or what I felt was bad really was working for my good especially for where I am now in leadership."

Table 12

Perception of Faced Barriers

Perceptual Barriers	Social Barriers	Personal Barriers
Anger	Disdain for Leadership	Emotional
Blame Other	Routine	Physical
Grudge	Rituals	Psychological
Self-Blame	Traditions	Spiritual
Self-Sabotage		
Settling - Adopting		

Participant 6 also spoke about the comfortability of people and traditional behaviors towards female Christian ministry leaders.

> Mainly putting too much focus on trying to gather everybody and gather everybody in making sure, people want to be apart, committed, and consistent. However, people are not there yet. They are comfortable where they are and they do not want to

mature or grow. I start slacking because I see myself going an extra mile for people that do not desire it. Wanting more leaders to come on board with doing what God requires. (Participant 6)

The response that is not aligned to theme 4 submitted by Participant 6 provided more insight are common actions of people and not necessarily a barrier for women in leadership. However, it did provide a concept to be studied in the future regarding non-leaders and their reactions to women in leadership. Theme 4 correlates and answers RQ4 listed below and shown in Table 13 are participants responses to Theme 4.

Table 13

Perceptions of Leadership

Theme 4	**Number of Participants**
Female Perception of Leadership	8
Response not aligned to the theme 4	1
Outlier	1

One hundred percent or 10 out of 10 participants have expressed perceived barriers because of tradition, religion, and previous experiences. Christian ministry leadership for women has encountered numerous of barriers for decades. However, the perceptions of barriers are the reality for women advancing up the career ladder. This is primarily due to cultural perceptions, cultural behaviors, and cultural diversity (Paustian-Underdahl et al., 2014). The purpose of this qualitative case study was to explore how women perceived and overcame social, cultural, and perceptual barriers to succeed as leaders in Christian ministry (Scott, 2010). Their behaviors have also challenged the set traditions and rituals by going beyond the norm and reaching for what they are purposed to do (Paustian-Underdahl et al., 2014).

Figure 10. Participants' expressions of perceived internal barriers.

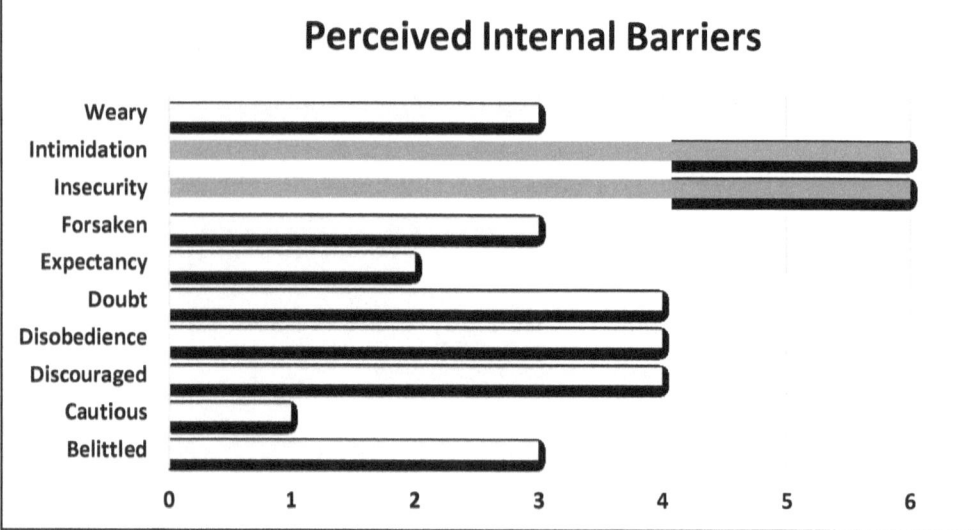

Participant 1 spoke about society has made traditional barriers a part of church routine.

> It has been rewarding from the standpoint of I know that is what God has me to do, but from the state of dealing with people it has been scary. You learn that not everybody is like-minded or secure in knowing I

> have been called to do a certain thing. Traditional barrier is a part of society. The societal barriers are set up and created within the church. The barriers can be a multiple of things. (Participant 1)

Participant 2 spoke about how people will surprise you and people can be a barrier for female Christian ministry leaders.

> I have had some bad experiences and some good one. I will say that the good ones have overtaken the bad ones. People are not who you think they are. People judge you. I live in a Flintstone land because I think everybody is good because of my heart. I believe everybody as a Christian should have that heart. I believe that you should make a change when you become a Christian. You should be God like. If I do not see it then I just pray or I back myself away. (Participant 2)

Participant 3 spoke about the emotions of being a female Christian ministry leader and how to be genuine regardless of the barriers faced.

> Enlightening, Positive, and Scary. I would say that my experience would be positive. I think it has a lot to do with the Heart that God has given us to do this. He gives us what we need to deal with all of this stuff. He gives us the heart to deal with the people in ministry that are not genuine or sincere, that is why it does not matter as much because God helps us deal with what we encounter because we are doing it for him. (Participant 3)

Participants 4 spoke about as a female Christian ministry leader being equipped and having confidence in that.

> I have learned a lot about me being a Christian Female Leader. I have felt better equipped to do what I need to do in the corporate world. My confidence level is very high there. I feel safe and secure verses how it is translated into what I do in ministry. I think the same skills should be easily translated. Maybe because I felt better equipped in the corporate world because I have a degree or I have certain experience

there, but I now understand that my whole life experience has been equipping me as a women leader for ministry. It took me some time to realize how to build that same level of confidence, but it has been an enlightening journey understanding that I am in God. I finally do not feel like I have to come from a certain pedigree or background or take a certain traditional path to get there. However, I am here simply because God called me I am already equipped and justified to be in this place and keeping my own voice as a female leader and not feeling like I had to ascribe to a certain voice. (Participant 4)

Participant 5 spoke about discrepancies regarding women in leadership climbing the ladder as an executive.

Despite an increased presence of female employees in mid-management positions, executive positions continue to be male dominated. Women are underrepresented in areas of governance, directorship, and executive leadership. The higher up

> the ladder you go the greater disparity between male and female wages. (Participant 5)

Participant 6 spoke about using the barriers as a growth process for female Christian ministry leaders.

> I embrace the barriers that I have faced as opportunities to find a solution, and an opportunity to grow better. There will always be mishaps and misunderstandings, but the goal is to keep the ultimate outcome within sight, and endeavor a way to accomplish that. This includes keeping the recommendations and values of others in mind. I always keep the team approach at the forefront of my mind, not embracing a title so much so, that I fail to keep the result of the outcome in mind. (Participant 6)

Participant 7 spoke about the limited mindsets that are cultivated in Christian ministry for females in leadership.

> Small minds, lack of faith, and sin have been a few of the barriers that have blocked Christian Ministries

> from collaboratively building relations outside of the four walls. The needs of others are always first at hand in my position. No matter how I feel or what I think, I have been commissioned to respond with the love of Christ. (Participant 7)

Participant 8 spoke about being hopeful for changes in the future for female Christian ministry leaders.

> Their needs are greater than those barriers, but as a ministry leader, following the leadership of my pastor, I respect him as a leader being led by God. I pray that there will be a change of heart one day, but in the meantime, I brainstorm other ways to help women like donating to charitable organizations. I have learned that giving does not have to be a part of a particular ministry. It can just be a part of an individual. (Participant 8)

Participant 9 spoke about the restrictions on female Christian ministry leaders on how they apply what God has called them to do.

> Many people will not take you serious as a leader. They believe that it is a man's place. Some people will not allow you to deliver the word from the pulpit. Certain places will only allow you to speak if it is a women's conference. It is getting better, but women still face many barriers. Barriers have decreased to a certain degree. People are more open, but there are still denominations that will not fully receive women. (Participant 9)

Participant 10 spoke about female Christian ministry leaders not being judged and change should be accepted.

> Today's society, the barriers that we are facing now, that are more important, would be to find a way of not judging others that do not appear like the traditional ways of many Christians that we grew up seeing in our society. It is very imperative for us to realize that there is always changed and nothing stays the same. We must embrace change in order for us to

move in the movement of today and the current times that we live in. (Participant 10)

Leadership momentum. Participant 2 spoke about how female Christian ministry leaders should fortify themselves against barriers.

> I get fearless and unstoppable because I remember the things that God has brought me through before and it helps me to fortify for what is coming and what will be next. It pushes me to pray more to seek God more and see what God is going to do next. It pushes me to do better. When opposition comes, it causes me to become relentless and want to overcome the obstacle. When I feel like the opposition is trying to tear me down or belittle me by attempting to step on me and keep me down it strengthens me to fight. (Participant 2)

Participant 3 spoke about how feeling as if there is a constant battle not to ignore what she is called to do.

> It initially makes me want to quit. I then get that second wind after revamping. It reminds me of a war and how there are times we fight small battles within the war. Then we rest, retreat, and get ready to fight again. (Participant 3)

Participant 4 found motivation in opposition. She said, "I am motivated and fearless because the opposition should have killed me when he had the chance because I am moving forward regardless."

Coping mechanisms. Participant 1 spoke about the importance of counsel, but female Christian ministry leaders must make certain it is wise counsel.

> Wise counsel. Find a counselor that can help you. There is safety in the multitude of counsel. God has more than one way to get things accomplished. Seek the soundness of others that are outside of the four walls of the church. God's people are everywhere. We have to be open to listen and discern God in every aspect imaginable. (Participant 1)

Participant 3 spoke about prayer and meditation being a coping mechanism along with reading the bible.

> Rest, regroup, and recalibrate. Going to a conference or trip. Try the Symphony. Introduce yourself to different types of things. Reading books on specific topics and journaling your thoughts. Meditation and quiet time. The Word of God. As well as mentorship from my Pastor and through prayer. (Participant 3)

Participant 4 spoke about the need for a mentor that is willing to work with a female Christian ministry leader.

> The collaborative relations work hand in hand if you are blessed with female Christian leaders that are willing to encourage you, lift you up, and mentor you. I believe that training, mentorship and development going into Christian leadership is important. (Participant 4)

Each of the five themes is interpreted in Chapter 5. Included in Chapter 5 are conclusions and recommendations. Included will also be discussions on findings and analysis significant to the findings. Further discussion includes the limitations of the study, recommendation for action, and recommendations for further study.

Although there are barriers that exist for female Christian ministry leaders, leadership career momentum exists as well with women being optimistic, hopeful, and an expanded vision.

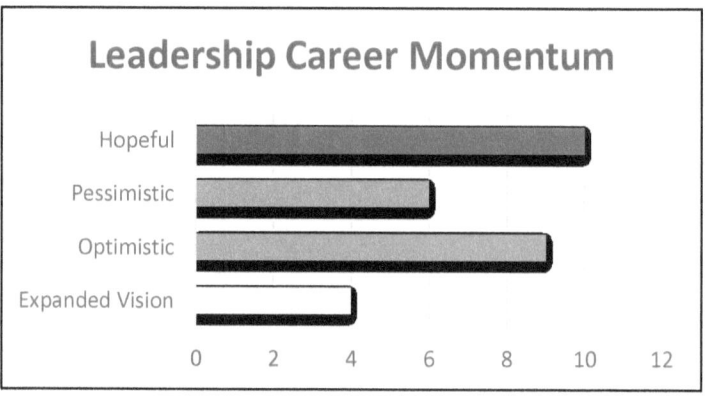

Figure 11. Participants' explanations of leadership career momentum.

Summary

The purpose of this qualitative case study was to explore how women perceived and overcame social, cultural, and perceptual barriers to succeed as leaders in

Christian ministry. A purposeful sample of 10 female Christian ministry leaders in the United States area was intentionally selected from various non-profit organizations. The selected targeted population was because of the barriers experienced in leadership positions as a woman in Christian ministry.

Each participant was asked 4 open ended questions. All interviews were audio taped. Data collected from the participants were transcribed ty the researcher and entered into NVivo 10 ® software. The researcher analyzed the data using a modified van Kam method by Moustakas (1994) and five themes emerged. Conveyed in Chapter 4 was the support for the five themes from the interviews. The five common themes resulted throughout the interview process were: (a) Female Perception of Leadership (b) Characteristics of Female Leadership (c) Internal and External Barriers (d) Leadership Momentum (e) Coping Mechanisms.

Chapter 5: Summary, Conclusions, and Recommendations

Introduction

Historically, gender has played a pivotal role in whether or not women receive Christian Ministry Leadership positions. The societal perception of women has been passed down through cultural teachings while misrepresenting female Christian ministry leaders (Vasavada, 2012). Women in leadership have not always been accepted due to tradition and cultural perceptions, regardless women should not eliminate their leadership assignments. (Bacha & Walker, 2013).

The purpose of this qualitative case study was to explore how women perceived and overcame social, cultural, and perceptual barriers to succeed as leaders in Christian ministry. (Ryan et al., 2011). The intent of Chapter 5 is to depict a greater understanding of the data analysis presented in Chapter 4. Chapter 5 features discussions on findings and analysis, significance of the findings, central research and 6 sub questions aligned to the themes, implications, limitations of the study, and recommendations for action. The chapter concludes with recommendations for further studies based on the findings in the current study.

Using a qualitative methodology with a qualitative case study design explored in the current study were the detailed, perceptions, accounts, and experience with the phenomenon of 10 female Christian ministry leaders (Yin, 2009). The purpose was to understand how women perceive their external and personal obstacles in Christian leadership. Further, this research revealed the social, culture, and perceptual barriers that women face when they seek Christian leadership positions and what some have done to overcome these barriers.

Face-to-face structured interviews were conducted using 4 open-ended questions. One hundred percent of the interviews were face to face. Interviews were audio taped and transcribed. Interviews lasted from a minimum of 45 minutes to a maximum of 2 hours. The four basic steps of used within this study are, one interview, and NVivo 10® data analysis software assisted in the organization and analysis of the transcribed data. Moustakas (1994) modified Van Kaam method was used to analyze the data. Emergent themes were developed from the transcribed and coded data.

Summary of the Study

The purpose of this qualitative case study was to explore how women perceived and overcame social, cultural, and perceptual barriers to succeed as leaders in Christian ministry. The internal, external, and self-perceived barriers that exist for women in Christian ministry leadership were examined through direct interaction with the participants (Johnson & Christensen, 2012). This study seeks to understand how women perceive their external and personal obstacles in Christian leadership. Further, this research revealed the social and self-perceptual barriers that women face when they seek Christian leadership positions and what some have done to overcome these barriers. It also identified inherent and learned characteristics necessary for

Christian leadership. For instance, according to Mento (2014), women in leadership nurture growth, a valuable asset to Christian leadership.

The purpose of this research is to reveal the personal, social, and perceptual barriers that women face when they seek Christian leadership positions (Scott, 2010). Secondly, to examine what measures women have taken to overcome these barriers (Michailidis et al., 2012). Thirdly, identify inherent and learned characteristics necessary for Christian leadership (Wienclaw, 2015) Servant leadership theory provides a base for understanding this phenomenon. Additionally, inclusive leadership provided a prospective that included diverse perceptions, but with the need to find and understand relatable common places to enhance the well-being of individuals, groups, and organizations (Jaworski, 2012).

While the percentage for Female Christian Ministry Leaders in nonprofit organizations has increased in recent years (Virick & Greer, 2012), women in leadership within

Christian ministry continues to fall significantly short of men in similar positions (Holst & Kirsch, 2015). The research identified the reasons for the shortage is due to barriers that still exist. Additionally, the research identifies that perceptions of women in leadership has not changed, but the perception of the women in leadership has progressed. The opportunities are limited for Female Christian Ministry Leaders and existing negative perceptions prevent women from securing a leadership position. The commitment and confidence in women as leaders remain entrenched in society and culture, which poses internal obstacles for women seeking leadership position in Christian ministry (Vasavada, 2012). The research identified that internal barriers exist because of culture and external barriers exist because of society. According to a study done on preparing women for leadership in Black Baptist churches, (Newkirk & Cooper, 2013) women who seek out leadership position in Christian ministry must deal with personal issues of sexism, financial struggles and oppression. The study further stated that women in Christian leadership would need to be fully prepared to deal with the common issues affecting churches, which might include spiritual, social, political, and economic issues. This study revealed that women in leadership deal with emotional, psychological, mental, and physical barriers. Additionally, this revealed where women in leadership experienced some situations that was shocking and unexpected. Newkirk and Cooper (2013) further found that "women who choose to embark in this profession face challenges and struggles, which their male counterparts often do not experience." This study identified that the social and culture barriers exist because the male counterpart do not accept women in leadership and the principles and standards are justified by manufactured protocols. As long as these barriers exist, women who seek to become Christian Ministry Leaders faced obstacles to reaching their goals. By examining the experiences of female Christian ministry, leaders who are or have been affected by external and personal barriers provided a basis for understanding what these barriers are, and how to overcome those barriers (Christian & Zippay, 2012). This study revealed that women are becoming motivated, fearless, and unstoppable. Women are learning how to maneuver around the barriers and become successful.

This study sought to understand how women perceived their external and personal obstacles in Christian leadership. Furthermore, this research revealed the social and self-perceptual barriers that women face when they seek Christian leadership positions and what some have done to overcome these barriers. It identified inherent and learned characteristics necessary for Christian leadership. For instance, according to Mento (2014), women in leadership nurture growth, a valuable asset to Christian leadership. However, this study will provide insight on those unique and inherent barriers that women face when seeking leadership roles in Christian ministry. This study revealed that women in leadership have learned through society and culture how to settle for less, adopt practices, and alter plans. Female specific strategies to success in Christian leadership despite the barriers were also being examined. (Newkirk & Cooper, 2013).

The purpose of this qualitative case study was to explore how women perceived and overcame social, cultural, and perceptual barriers to succeed as leaders in Christian ministry (Scott, 2010). Secondly, to examine what measures women have taken to overcome these barriers (Michailidis et al., 2012). The third one is to identify inherent and learned characteristics necessary for Christian leadership (Wienclaw, 2015) Servant leadership theory provided a base for understanding this phenomenon. Additionally, inclusive leadership also provided a prospective that included diverse perceptions, but with the need to find and understand relatable common places to enhance the well-being of individuals, groups, and organizations (Jaworski, 2012).

While there is ample literature that explored female Christian ministry leaders, this study examined an area that has been under represented in literature, i.e., how women perceive the constraints and their own leadership abilities. (Johns, 2013).

The foundation of this study was Servant leadership, Inclusive leadership that defined the need of leaders that are willing to serve, and female leaders are inclusive of all without bias, discrimination, or prejudice. The research of the study extended both theories because it provided a strategy or strategies that helped female Christian ministry leaders to overcome barriers and be in Christian ministry.

Significance of the Study

The significance of this study is to examine the experiences and perceptions of female Christian ministry leaders and to identify what barriers exist, because of social, cultural, and personal perceptions (Bowles, 2014). This research explored the steps that female Christian ministry leaders have taken to overcome some barriers and discovered a strategy to decrease or eliminate existing barriers in Christian ministry. This study identified coping mechanisms that can assist women in Christian ministry to succeed. Meditation, prayer, relaxation, counseling, mentoring, and conferences are all identified as ways to cope with barriers and be successful as a female Christian ministry leader. Women in leadership may possess the necessary education, training, and development to lead within Christian ministry however; they must remove barriers to be successful (Herrera et al., 2012). The research also revealed that the female Christian ministry leaders have 3 plus years of experience and educational experience up to a Master's Degree.

This study added to the current literature by analyzing the respondent's perceptions regarding internal and external barriers to leadership, steps women have taken to overcome barriers, and why they persevere despite obstacles. It was not known how women perceived and overcame social, cultural, and perceptual barriers to succeed as leaders in Christian ministry. Examining female Christian ministry leaders' experiences with internal and external barriers provided a basis for understanding what these barriers are, and how to negate those barriers (Christian & Zippay, 2012). This study seeks to understand how women perceived their personal obstacles in Christian leadership.

Furthermore, this research revealed the personal, social, and perceptual barriers that women face when they seek Christian leadership positions and what some have done to overcome these barriers. It also identified inherent and learned characteristics necessary for Christian leadership. Therefore, this study provided insight and strategy on these barriers. A recommendation was developed as to how women in leadership can be successful despite the barriers (Newkirk & Cooper, 2013). Practical application from this study provided valuable insight for women who are seeking Christian leadership positions, identified unknown barriers, and examined the experiences of female Christian ministry leaders to establish a strategy to overcome and attain the position they aspire.

Summary of Findings and Conclusions

Five themes emerged from the current study as conveyed in Chapter 4 was the support for the five themes from the interviews, questionnaires, and journal field notes. The five common themes resulted throughout the research process were: (a) Female Perception of Leadership (b) Characteristics of Female Leadership (c) Internal and External Barriers (d) Leadership Momentum (e) Coping Mechanisms.

The participants described barriers that women face as a leader in Christian ministry, as a common effect consistent with struggles of internal and external barriers. Additionally, the participants described internal barriers as having to deal with internal challenges from within. Some internal barriers identified are intimidation, insecurity, and fear, and rejection, defeat, discouraged, belittled, weary, and forsaken. The participants described external barriers as things that seemingly are beyond self-control. The participants' years in ministry ranged from 3 to 10 years.

Eighty percent of the participants expressed gratefulness for the opportunity to lead in Christian ministry. All participants worked in a non-profit organization, such as a church, and served as a leader in Christian ministry. Twenty percent of the participants also held leadership positions within the community as a community liaison, community advocate, women's ministry within the confines of a non-profit organization.

While the percentage for Female Christian Ministry Leaders in nonprofit organizations has increased in recent years (Virick & Greer, 2012), women in leadership within Christian ministry continues to fall significantly short of men in similar positions (Holst & Kirsch, 2015). The opportunities are limited for Female Christian Ministry Leaders and existing negative perceptions prevent women from securing a leadership position. The commitment and confidence in women as leaders remain entrenched in society and culture, which poses internal obstacles for women seeking leadership in Christian ministry (Vasavada,

2012). According to a study done on preparing women for leadership in Black Baptist churches (Newkirk & Cooper, 2013) women who seek out leadership in Christian ministry must deal with personal issues of sexism, financial struggles, and oppression. The study further stated that women in Christian leadership would need to be fully prepared to deal with the common issues affecting churches, which might include spiritual, social, political, and economic issues. Newkirk and Cooper (2013) further found that "women who choose to embark in this profession face challenges and struggles, which their male counterparts often do not experience." As long as these barriers exist, women who seek to become Christian Ministry Leaders faced obstacles to reaching their goals.

Women in leadership may possess the necessary education, training, and development to lead within Christian ministry however; they must remove barriers to be successful (Herrera et al., 2012). Opportunities for female Christian ministry leaders have increased over the decades and the nonprofit organizations have been helpful in giving women the opportunity to exercise their leadership abilities. Women have the opportunity to balance career and ministry while holding leadership positions in Christian ministry. The opportunity to serve others is the priority of female Christian ministry leaders.

Mento (2014) believes that nonprofit organizations, including those related to Christian ministry, are actually hindered by not having women in leadership roles. Women have innate abilities to nurture growth. Nonprofits like a Christian ministry recognize the need to serve others within the community.

The societal perception of women has been passed down through cultural teachings while misrepresenting female Christian ministry leaders (Vasavada, 2012). Women in leadership have not always been accepted due to tradition and cultural perceptions, regardless women should not eliminate their leadership assignments. (Bacha & Walker, 2013). Additionally, discussion was regarding the cultural behaviors of women in various leadership positions have learned to adapt and adopt many of the cultural perceptions. Their behaviors have also challenged the set traditions and rituals by going beyond the norm by reaching for what they are purposed to do (Paustian-Underdahl et al., 2014).

Inclusive of cultural perception and cultural behaviors, a continued discussion of cultural barriers examined a training tool for women in leadership to gain knowledge and influence in Christian ministry (Vevere, 2014). Gender diversity in leadership examines female Christian ministry leaders are influencing the nature of diversity and women in leadership are fostering relationships between diversity, Christian ministry, and society (Virick & Greer, 2012). Gender differences within certain organization are classified by a variety of metaphors, that signify biases and discriminatory obstacles that hinder women in leadership (Smith et al., 2012).

The findings from the theme internal and external barriers could assist leadership within Christian ministry to understand the perceptions of women in leadership and find ways to eliminate the barriers that exist. Further insight may be beneficial to male leaders to understand from a theoretical perspective how the behaviors are affecting the overall success of Christian ministry and provide insight to the female Christian ministry leaders' ways to succeed if the barriers will not be diminished.

> The church, society, or the community has not done the best job at representing Jesus and His mission to the world. The needs of others are what makes ministry necessary and worth the effort to push past barriers. In order to continue to make an impact, women of faith must press forward despite times of being misunderstood in the marketplace and marginalized inside the church. (Participant 1)

Participant 3 noted:

> I had a vision that leadership loved but it was not acknowledged right away. It appeared to have been ignored until finally the leadership found time to

review what I had submitted. God was telling me to get it done prior to a certain time but I was waiting on approval from male leadership. I have learned that when you obey God everything will fall into place. I felt like it was a barrier because I was waiting on him to approve it but he never did. However, as I continued to move forward anyway the male leader finally came around. I learned that the barrier was good because it was not for that particular location because it would have put limitations on it. We hinder ourselves because we are waiting on an approval from a man. (Participant 3)

Participant 8 said:

> I am being stretched out of my comfort zone because it is forcing me to be out front when I would just like to be unnoticed. I deal with my own self-insecurities prior to even meeting face to face with those that are imposed upon me from external sources. (Participant 8)

Participant 9 stated:

> My largest barrier would be expectancy; expectancy of myself and the expectations from others. So many people expect so many different things from me. I am expected to do everything right. It makes me feel like I have not been walking in what God wanted me to do. I will not do any more facades or portray anything other than who God has called me to be. I expect to do the will of God. Whoever understands or do not understand. It is my expectation to walk into what I am called to do. (Participant 9)

Women in Christian leadership will need to be fully prepared to deal with the common issues affecting churches, which might include spiritual, social, political, and economic issues. Newkirk and Cooper (2013) further found that "women who choose to embark in this profession face challenges and struggles, which their male counterparts often do not experience." As long as these barriers exist, women who seek to become Christian Ministry Leaders faced obstacles to reaching their goals. By examining the experiences of female Christian ministry, leaders who are or have been affected by external and personal barriers provided a basis for understanding what these barriers are, and how to overcome those barriers (Christian & Zippay, 2012).

As a Christian leader the individual disciplines and practices that are routinely done has the greatest influence on a Christian leader's preference. It is during the disciplined rituals of meditation, evaluation, prayer, journaling, and cultivation that leaders can clearly discern the direction of God and position themselves to follow those directions (Crowley, 2014). Formational worship is the time that Christian leaders are built, restored, and their capacity increases to meet the needs of others (Noland, 2009). It is impossible to provide needed support to others when the leader themselves are not in a place to do so. Without the influence of formational worship, Christian leaders can be lacking or become deficient and will not have the ability to carry out the plans of God. Formational worship also influences the desire of the leader to want more and to do more for God and for Gods people (Scott, 2010). It is an intimate time that God pours into the Christian leader through training, development, enlightenment, and inspiration to do what is required of them. Formational worship removes the want to be selfish or have self-absorbed feelings that result into self-willed actions. Likewise, formational worship influences Christian leaders so that Christian leaders can have a positive influence on others. What is done in the private times of formational worship can then is productive in corporate time.

Formational worship influences a Christian leader's preference in leadership theory by how effective the leader was and is. As a Christian leader the individual disciplines and practices that are routinely done has the greatest influence on a Christian leader's preference. It is during the disciplined rituals of meditation, evaluation, prayer, journaling, and cultivation that leaders can clearly discern the direction of God and position themselves to follow those directions (Crowley, 2014).

The findings of the theme, coping mechanisms suggest that women leaders can find a way to advance as a leader in Christian ministry by applying the coping techniques of a servant leader. The ability for female Christian ministry leaders to cope with internal and external barriers benefited the followers to be served appropriately and with substance. Applying different ways to cope with barriers will help both the leader and followers.

Participants revealed in interviews that the best coping mechanisms by experience are (a) prayer and having a conversation with God; (b) meditation and guidance; (c) counseling and wise counsel; (d) rest, retreat, and relaxation. The majority if not all of the participants believe that there is no way a leader in Christian ministry can face barriers without the above coping mechanisms, but specifically those who are female Christian ministry leaders.

Additionally, collaboration amongst the leader, followers, and other leaders enables support from the leader to the follower and from the follower to the leader. Both participants become encourages and enablers of one another to reach their ultimate potential. The overall characteristics of Servant Leadership are leaders are not selfish but selfless (Robert Greenleaf, 1977). The common elements of effective Leadership are serving others, establishing relationships, and influence (Doh & Quigley, 2014). Leadership is assessed by the effectiveness of service to render to others without forsaking oneself.

> I am learning to deal with me, the internal and allow God to deal with the external. The participants believe that the best coping mechanisms are prayer, medication, and wise counsel. Some of the participants have found that having collaboration with other female leaders and mentorship are also beneficial for coping with internal and external challenges. Participants also included that relaxing,

> regrouping, and taking a retreat can give your mind, emotions, and physical body a needed break. (Participant 4)

Participant 1 noted:

> Wise counsel. Finding a counselor that can help me be successful. There is safety in the multitude of counsel. God has more than one way to get things accomplished. I seek the soundness of others that are outside of the four walls of the church. God's people are everywhere. We have to be open to listen and discern God in every aspect imaginable. I think it is crucial to develop relationship with God so you can hear His voice and His directions. (Participant 1)

Participant 2 added:

> Prayer and just talking to God. Having a conversation with God is important. You do not have to be all loud or deep but just having a conversation with God throughout the day or while you are driving in your car. Pray with expectations and knowing that

God can handle any situation. Pray for God to bless you also, regardless of the barriers that are being faced. (Participant 2)

A leader is someone who exercises authority over other people. Leadership entails being in charge of other people in multiple ways. It consists of influencing, motivating, organizing, and coordinating the work of others (Chin & Sanchez-Hucles, 2007).

History has contended that women did not possess the qualifications or characteristics to lead (McBride, 2011). Society and culture opposed women being assertive enough to be in a *leader*ship positions (Ochoa, 2011). However, according to C.E. Washington (2010), female Christian ministry leaders can succeed when equipped with proper training, mentorship, and education. Women have the knowledge, skills, and ability to be a leader in Christian ministry. Christian ministry has traditionally been dominated by men and social mores have opposed women in these leadership positions (Forbes, 2011).

As the leader take note of how the followers have reached a necessary point in the plan, improvements integrated carefully into the overall scheme are critical for leaders to be relentless and remain focused. Improvements are an incentive for followers and thus followers received rewards for the hard work and input. (Benson, 2015) addresses the assessment of behaviors before and the behaviors after the changes and most importantly the change model includes every participant involved.

Learned behaviors have taught women to adopt and settle for barriers that are presented by culture, social, and personal barriers. Women in various leadership positions have learned to adapt and adopt many of the cultural perceptions. Their behaviors have also challenged the set traditions and rituals by going beyond the norm by reaching for what they are purposed to do (Paustian-Underdahl et al., 2014). Cultural barriers have become a training tool for women in leadership to gain knowledge and influence in Christian ministry (Vevere, 2014). Cultural behaviors of women are a learned or adopted attitude that enables uncertain behaviors that are relative to pleasing the traditions of culture. Each culture has its own individualistic concept regarding female Christian ministry leaders and it does not contribute to benefit the nonprofit organization. A more in-depth concept is cultural behaviors are not just specific to an individual person, but it includes groups with particular perspective regarding female Christian ministry leaders. Cultural behaviors are concepts used to make decisions that cause a certain behavior without consulting other groups for understanding (Rogers, 2010).

Leaders have to adapt to the things of the world but not adopt the things of the world. We adapt to function in a world that is full of different perspectives that engage many different behaviors. However, through understanding, tolerance, and love those behaviors can be transformed. Tolerance is having patience with other beliefs and not humanly being an opposition, but spiritually abiding in truth and love (Carson, 2012).

Characteristics of female leaders demonstrate the relentless behaviors of 80% of the participants. The participants were motivated and strengthened with each barrier that was encountered. Although, the barriers were present to stop progress the participants felt the need to keep moving forward without fear and hesitation. However, 20% of the participants admitted to just wanting to take a step back and wanting to quit at times.

> I get fearless and unstoppable because I remember the things that God has brought me through before and it helps me to fortify for what is coming and what will be next. It pushes me to pray more to seek God more and see what God is going to do next. It pushes me to do better. When opposition comes, it causes me to become relentless and want to overcome the obstacle. When I feel like the opposition is trying to tear me down or belittle me by attempting to step on me and keep me down it strengthens me to fight. My overall experience is good. Because I am, mature and

seasoned because I was mentored by older women that trained me. (Participant 2)

Participant 4 said:

I am motivated and fearless because the opposition should have killed me when he had the chance because I am moving forward regardless. This journey has been a very long learning experience through the tears, friction, and rejection that comes with being a Christian Ministry leader, as a woman because now I know just how much God loves me, and just how much I have to offer someone else. Participant 5 stated, I use to look at being a woman leader in Christian ministry as a negative thing, but I am now changing my outlook to view it more of a positive aspect. (Participant 4)

Despite this need for leaders in Christian ministry, the opportunity is not always available to women because social, cultural, and perceptual barriers block their entry into these roles (Virick & Greer, 2012). Christian ministry is a sacrificial service to carry out the commission of God here on earth. Women have taken steps to become capable leaders through education, training, and development to meet the expectations of being a Christian ministry leader. Mento (2014) believes that nonprofit organizations, including those related to Christian ministry, are actually hindered by not having women in leadership roles. Women have innate abilities to nurture growth. Nonprofits like a Christian ministry recognize the need to serve others within the community. This may drive change regardless of constraints presented by society and culture about women (Skelly & Johnson, 2011).

    Social non-business interaction is to remove the tension and allow individuals and groups within the organization to be comfortable. Social non-business interaction can identify what stimulates individuals or groups to produce at full capacity. When people are not open and comfortable with sharing, collaborating, or being in a team they tend to hold back. Social non-business interaction provides time for diverse people, with diverse cultures to interact with one another. There are some instances where problems can arise, however problems arise every day and part of understanding one another is learning how to relate to each other even when problems exist. One concern the organization could possibly have is if confusion enters the workplace from a non-business social event. Cultural preferences most significantly influence the social interaction style of an organization because of tradition and what is traditional accepted within each diverse culture.

The perception is leaders must have a vision and women are not visionaries. If a woman represents qualities of leadership, some cultures perceive it as a violation. The stereotype leads to a belief that women leaders are not needed or respected. Similar to Dzubinski (2012) and Bush (2012), Cook (2010), agrees with the negative perception that has penetrated the minds of people regarding female Christian ministry leaders. Bush (2012) differently uses the term multicultural, which pertains to the diversity of cultures to include gender, race, and culture. However, similar to Dzubinski (2012), culture is a major element of diversity and distinguishes what is acceptable. Dzubinski (2012) identified the culture, environment, and nature within the expectations of leadership.

The individual and personal thoughts of a leader do not supersede the needs of others. Although the intent is to have a personal belief system that does not necessarily affect others, the reality is beliefs turn into patterns of behavior. Cultural barriers are not an advocate of group integration, bonding, or connecting to anything that stood in the way of personal advancement.

Leadership that is accountable and trustworthy exceeds cultural preferences, traditions, and barriers to inspire. Servant leadership motivates, cultivate standards, approaches, and actions for individuals and groups and the organization as a whole. (Greenleaf, 1977). Their behaviors have also challenged the set traditions and rituals by going beyond the norm by reaching for what they are purposed to do (Paustian-Underdahl et al., 2014).

Ninety percent of participants expressed a disdain for leadership, but just as relevant, the participants have all experienced the routine barriers that are evident through perceptual, social, and personal barriers. The participants have dealt with emotional, physical, psychological, and spiritual barriers that do not easily go away. The participants voiced a need to place blame on others and self because of being seemingly forced to accept or adopt routines, rituals, and traditions that constrain the participant from leading effectively. Additionally, the participant's perceptions are stained by emotional, physical, psychological, and spiritual barriers. As a result, participants have admitted to holding resentments against male leadership and have caused self-sabotage by not yielding to directives given.

> I did not realize the emotional, psychological, and spiritual struggles I would encounter when we (my husband and I) started the ministry that as my

husband and I equally doing things professionally together is different in ministry. Women or wives are not considered equal in ministry but are held just as accountable. Men do not want women to speak or say anything. As a woman, I am trying to be better in ministry but better may not what most ministries or men desire for women. There is an inconsistency and my struggle is with being who God has called me to be and who man tries to force me to be. (Participant 4)

Participant 7 said:

I feel like my issues are within myself and with others because I work in a male dominated field. Working with a staff that are older than I am and do not provide a certain level of respect. As a woman I am questioned when I give directives even though I am a leader. They have to check with the men before they accept my directives. I am affected internally where I question my ability. I constantly have to tell myself that I have the ability to do this. (Participant 7)

Andronoviene (2013) argues that women have the qualities necessary for leadership. With training, development, and coaching women recently are experiencing the respect and encouragement deserved as a leader. Additionally, women have the ability to achieve standards but also lead vigorously presenting excellence as a standard. Women lead with more passion and fervency with the tools provided such as education, mentorship and coaching (Andronoviene, 2013). Newkirk and Cooper (2013) differently discusses that mentorship is not adequate, but an individual in leadership should receive a formal theological education. England (2011) is in agreement with Andronoviene and Newkirk concerning the importance of mentorship. However, Newkirk and Cooper (2013) and England (2011) similarly to Andronoviene (2013) communicate that mentorship and internships are necessary for preparing women in leadership. Similar to Andronoviene

(2013), Newkirk and Cooper (2013) uses a professional analogy of a medical student that trains and receives a degree so must women in leadership.

The subject of qualification, standards, and passion of women in leadership provided by Andronoviene (2013) give a significant and substantial view of the need for women in leadership. Newkirk & Cooper (2013) expresses the importance of effective leadership particularly women in ministry as being just as important as the careers as those in the medical profession. England (2011) discusses the order or headship within the Bible and the areas for women to assist in the church, but indicates the need for women leaders in the church. The methods, within the research, are sturdy and provide definition. Andronoviene (2013) describes practice as an activity that an individual willing participation whether complex or simple. During the process, the individual realizes the need for a standard of excellence. Newkirk & Cooper (2013) also expresses the difficulty faced for women in leadership, but mentors can help women operate in success. Andronoviene (2013) mentions finding creative ways of leadership for women and although that is an idea to ponder, the gap remains of the quality in the path that women take to leadership.

The perception of a leader is the understanding of what is right, wrong, fair, and morally correct, which has nothing to do with gender. A female Christian ministry leader has the ability to meet the guidelines when decisions are made according to the overall benefit of serving in Christian ministry and eliminates the need to benefit self. When society removes biases, prejudices, and discriminations, people are able to view leadership from a broader prospective and adapt to a global mindset without defense or offense (Bacha & Walker, 2013). The leader's ability to exert power, influence, and authority effectively depends upon the understanding of cultural differences and the ability to gain the respect level of other leaders and the followers.

Some cultures relate power to dominance or being able to dictate to an individual or group without explanation or collaboration (Ott, 2011). In other cultures, power represents the ability to mobilize and activate people, things, and groups without force or coercion. Similar to power, authority is perceived in various cultures as only one individual having the control to determine what is right or wrong and any other contribution is acceptable (Marsh, 2013). However, there are cultures that view authority as the ability to receive consultation from a leader that is deemed as a respected expert and the expert opinion of the leader weighs heavier in decision making. Just as power and authority dictate the different perceptions of what is ethical in leadership influence has a great effect as well. Influence in many cultures signifies respect earned by a leader through motivation, inspiration, and the ability of the leader to make an impact (Vevere, 2014). Leaders with great influence appreciated for guidance, direction, and instruction, which are viewed similar in most cultures. Leaders without influence experience less production, effort, and vitality within an organization. Culture shapes an organization through leadership, but leadership must have power, influence, and authority in order to see productive results.

> It has been rewarding from the standpoint of I know that is what God has me to do, but from the state of dealing with people it has been scary. You learn that not everybody is like-minded or secure in knowing I have been called to do a certain thing. Traditional barrier is a part of society. The societal barriers are set up and created within the church. The barriers can be a multiple of things. (Participant 1)

Participant 6 said:

> I embrace the barriers that I have faced as opportunities to find a solution, and an opportunity to grow better. There will always be mishaps and misunderstandings, but the goal is to keep the ultimate outcome within sight, and endeavor a way to accomplish that. This includes keeping the

recommendations and values of others in mind. I always keep the team approach at the forefront of my mind, not embracing a title so much so, that I fail to keep the result of the outcome in mind. (Participant 6)

Participant 10 added:

Today's society, the barriers that we are facing now, that are more important, would be to find a way of not judging others that do not appear like the traditional ways of many Christians that we grew up seeing in our society. It is very imperative for us to realize that there is always changed and nothing stays the same. We must embrace change in order for us to move in the movement of today and the current times that we live in. (Participant 10)

This research has added to existing research by identifying known and unknown barriers through experiences with suggested coping mechanisms that are successful for female Christian ministry leaders (Michailidis et al., 2012). Additionally, the research has added to the previous research the social, personal, and perceptual barriers that can be addressed with current and future leadership to eliminate nurturing barriers within an organization (Scott, 2010). Previous research shows that biases and discrimination exists in general and it has identified the women are in the majority as recipients to such actions (Doh & Quigley, 2014).

Implications

The results of this research can be utilized for Christian ministry leaders in nonprofit organizations to establish new norms, practices, and perspectives of society, culture, and tradition. Included in the category of society, culture, and traditions are the individual participants, which would be the smaller scale of implication. The research implies that changes are necessary from within or internally of individuals and groups, which would stimulate change that extends externally to penetrate cultures. According to Servant Leadership and Inclusive Leadership theory, it is every individual leader's purpose to serve others in a selfless fashion. Serving others is inclusive of all and is not limited to perception or certain groups. Serving others is selfless, but turns into selfishness when leadership intentionally and purposefully employs external obstructions of biases and discrimination. This study identified internal and external barriers that can be dealt with on an individual level and a global level. Inclusive leadership accepts the contributions of all that are willing to serve and give of themselves for the betterment of others. Inclusion encompasses all levels of the organization, being a valued contributor and being fully responsible for your contribution to the ultimate result (Fierke et al., 2014).

Theoretical implications. Servant leadership theory and inclusive leadership theory provided a base for understanding the phenomenon. Servant leadership, according to Greenleaf (1977), is a natural desire of each person, an innate feeling moving one to lead and serve rather than be lead and served. Thus if servant leadership is innate then one should be able to perceive it at many levels. Servant leadership implies to all genders that have a desire to serve others. It is not predicated on a male or female. External barriers create and nurture internal barriers. Internal barriers were perceived by the participants as results formed because of a negative experience that was self-imposed or experienced by others. External barriers were perceived by the participants as actions taken that are beyond an individual or groups control. The participants expressed the depth of internal and external barriers that are present while being a female Christian ministry leader and are dealing with internal barriers of insecurity, intimidation, doubt, fear, and uncertainty. Also voiced were times of discouragement and weariness from dealing with the external barriers of men that desire to disapprove of a woman as a leader. Although the participants have sacrificed greatly for others, it was questioned whether the sacrifices being made were even worth it. The expectations of society, culture, and perceptions are perceived as forms of abandonment. The theory of inclusive leadership has not been experienced and the participants have a disdain for leadership with feelings of disapproval, unacceptance, and being at a disadvantage compared to the male leader in Christian ministry. Controls and limits have been established as a set order or protocol to keep women in leadership at a certain level.

Although, traditional and cultural perceptions attempt to limit female Christian ministry leaders to serve, the natural desire of a person pushes women to lead regardless of the barriers that are faced (Greenleaf, 1977). Additionally, inclusive leadership provided a prospective that included diverse perceptions, which include both male and female leadership (Fierke et al., 2014). The drive to find and understand relatable common places enhances the well-being of individuals, groups, and organizations (Jaworski, 2012). The foundation for Christian ministry is servant leadership often times its weakness is allowing tradition, society, and culture to override the principle of servant leadership and inclusive leadership theories (Ross, 2015).

Since, Servant Leadership does not discriminate or use biases regarding serving others then there should be no discrimination or biases for the women desiring to serve others.

Practical implications. Barriers will always exist just as change will always be evident. Therefore, the key to being a successful female Christian ministry leader is identifying those barriers and knowing which barriers are within an individual's control to change (Newkirk & Cooper, 2013). If female Christian ministry leaders would be vigilant about addressing the areas of intimidation, insecurity, and fear regardless of what is happening externally success can still be achieved (Holst & Kirsch, 2015). Of course, the reality is that changing the perception of culture, society, and tradition is a long transition (Lambert & Lambert, 2012). Leaders must be accountable to do self-evaluations to examine areas of improvement. Internal barriers can be dealt with and eliminated with discipline and studious attention (Vasavada, 2012). The realities of external barriers are not always as simple to confiscate. Although, it is practical for barriers to exist both internally and externally for individuals and organizations, how the barriers are dealt with brings a reality to the service leadership and inclusive leadership (Newkirk & Cooper (2013).

Each theory involves people that make choices and decisions that are not always favorable for others. There are organizations that are closing down for the mere fact they are not being real world and applying ethical relevance (Donaldson, 1996). Sometimes it may take changing some things but it is worth it and it is something that must be done in order to be able to give a guarantee (Skelly & Johnson, 2011). It cannot be a seasonal or periodic episode, but it must be constant for every participant of the organization especially leadership (Dahlvig & Longman, 2010). The only true way to guarantee organization viability is to adhere to fair and just guidelines set forth and when error is made quickly correct it (Fifer, 2015). As women in Christian ministry, there have always been barriers and barriers will continue to be (Tidball, 2012). The realization is that women in Christian ministry cannot allow the barriers to stop individual or group success. Female Christian ministry leaders know first-hand by experience the effects that barriers have emotionally, physically, mentally, psychologically, and spiritually (Bryant-Anderson & Roby, 2012). Knowing first hand means that female Christian ministry leaders can be the change that is necessary to see a difference.

Future implications. From this study, it is clear that further research could be conducted to find ways to enhance or change the perceptions of society and expand the traditions of culture (Bacha & Walker, 2013). Christian ministry can take an active role in establishing traditions that are acceptable to including all people for serving others. The protocol could be for Christian ministry leaders to adopt the tradition of serving all and all be served equally and fairly without biases and discrimination (Michailidis et al., 2012). The study found that the majority of barriers come from within, such as insecurity, intimidation, fear, abandonment, and control, which is primarily because of external barriers such as tradition, culture, and society (Doh & Quigley, 2014). If external barriers are diminished, then internal barriers can be decreased. However, the reality is that barriers will never go away (Chen et al., 2014). The study identified ways of coping with various barriers for female Christian ministry leaders such as prayer, medication, retreats, mentoring, and education (Crowley, 2014). As leaders, we are bound to serve regardless of the individual, but choose those that are able to serve. Service and inclusion are selfless and sacrificial according to (McLeskey & Waldron, n.d.). The theories of servant leadership and inclusive leadership are both needed in Christian ministry. Equally so the leaders should be held accountable for demonstrating both. Christian ministry leaders being held accountable will change the environment and culture of Christian ministry (Forbes, 2011). The culture within all organizations specifically Christian ministry lives and cultivates based on the leadership. The future study could interview both male and female to compare the perceptions of both and define the differences. It is the difference of perception that a common place could be found (GuideStar, 2011). Theoretically, both male and female perceive things differently. Many things that are being perceived on both sides deal with traditional experiences that each one of them can changed by the individuals and the organizations.

The researcher must approach data collection avoiding any prejudgments, diminish bias, and without discrimination while experiencing the data as if for the first time (Moustakas, 1994). Having some knowledge of the female Christian ministry leadership, the researcher had to abstain from any prejudgments or bias in order to ensure that the data were not tainted in form. The focus of the study was on female Christian ministry leaders in the United States nonprofit organizations. Perceptions of the experiences expressed by the 10 participants in the study do not adequately represent the perceptions of all female Christian ministry leaders' women leaders in nonprofit organizations. A final limitation that could have a direct impact on the interpretations of the findings is the reliance upon the honesty of the responses expressed by each participant while describing their lived experiences as a female Christian ministry leader in a nonprofit organization.

Recommendations

The findings found in this research contain valuable insight into the phenomenon of how women in leadership perceive their experiences as leaders, how they explain their own learned and inherent characteristics, why they persevere in this profession, and how they contend with barriers in Christian ministry. Five themes emerged. The findings are consistent with the themes and influence the following recommendations for future research. Each recommendation is tied to a specific finding from my study and links are made below.

Recommendations for future research. Throughout this research, potential areas of future study developed. This study was significant because it identified (a) the cultural, social, and perceptual barriers that women face when they seek Christian leadership positions, (b) examine what measures women have taken to overcome these barriers and be successful. Five recommendations for future research emerged during the analysis of evidence.

1. Replicate this research study in other types of organizations or groups. This research focused on one nonprofit organization located in the United States.

2. A quantitative analysis can be conducted of organizational culture and leadership styles among other for profit leaders across different business ventures, such as in the field of education, medical, and government. Compare and contrast similarities and differences that materialize.

3. In addition to quantitative analysis, a qualitative, phenomenological study of male leaders' perception of women in leadership may offer insight to a gap of why barriers still exist.

4. Within nonprofit organizations, female Christian ministry leaders in this study received years of education and training. A replication of this study could include how organizational structural hierarchy influences the placement of degreed female Christian ministry leaders. For example, (Washington, 2010), female Christian ministry leaders can succeed when equipped with proper training, mentorship, and education. A strategy for

success can lead to breakthroughs for women, although the remaining perceptions of women as lacking the right qualities for this type of leadership can present areas of discomfort, challenges, and barriers (Nwoye, 2011).

5. The researcher focused on servant leadership theory and inclusive leadership theory as a base for understanding the structure of Christian ministry and the hierarchy of a nonprofit organization. Bacha & Walker (2013) suggests the removal of biases, prejudices, and discriminations, people can view leadership from a broader prospective and adapt to a global mindset, which is to find similarities, adopt new practices, and adapt to new processes.

Christian ministry has a hierarchal structure, and women who seek leadership positions and cultural styles form the perception of what is considered a good leader, especially in making decisions. Some cultures relate power to dominance or being able to dictate to an individual or group without explanation or collaboration (Ott, 2011). It concurs that social, cultural, and perceptual barriers still currently exist for female Christian ministry leaders. A valuable method to include to cultural perceptions, cultural behaviors, and cultural diversity is flexibility (Ruiz-Jimenez & Fuentes-Fuentes, 2016). History and the literature continue to express the social, cultural, and perceptual barriers that support bias, discrimination, and preferences (Paustian-Underdahl, Walker, & Woehr, 2014). The strengths of the study was being able to interview female Christian ministry leaders face to face, experiencing their behaviors, facial expressions, gestures, and emotions, and able to provide a sense of hope and encouragement for each participant. However, the weakness of the study is it was truly an emotional experience and many things spoken were from an emotional place of hurt.

Recommendations for future practice. This study has unlocked the access for further study with regard to Christian ministry and nonprofit organizations. The researcher suggests two recommendations for future practice. The first recommendation involves a crucial assessment and evaluation of leadership intentions and motives within nonprofit organizations concerning the importance of perception and changing traditions of society and culture. The second recommendation focuses the role of leadership to bring change to nonprofit organization in Christian ministry.

1. Mento (2014) suggests that nonprofit organizations, including those related to Christian ministry, are actually hindered by not having women in leadership roles. Women have innate abilities to nurture growth. Nonprofit organizations like a Christian ministry recognize the need to serve others within the community. This may originate change regardless of constraints presented by society and culture about women (Skelly & Johnson, 2011). Cultural barriers have become a training tool for women in leadership to gain knowledge and influence in Christian ministry (Vevere, 2014). Cultural behaviors of women are a learned or adopted attitude that enables uncertain behaviors that are relative to pleasing the traditions of culture. For example, Benson (2015) addresses the need for assessments of behaviors before change takes place and the behaviors after the changes are implemented specifically for leaders because leaders set the tone for an organization. Additionally, Christian ministry leaders may contemplate conducting group surveys or group interviews, which could provide a collaborative process where expectations are shared quickly. In the perspective of constructing changes in behavior, this could substantiate to be useful if change is the goal (Rogers, 2010).

2. Leaders in nonprofit organizations should take the time to examine their organizational behaviors with the intention to understand how it influences social, cultural, and perceptual

barriers for women. Leaders need to learn how to promote inclusive ways to increase acceptance, mutual respect, expand the potential for female Christian ministry leaders (Beaty & Davis, 2012). The Benson (2015) change model could assist in establishing respect and flexibility regarding the different views will require the most important communication tool, which is listening. The organization and leader must be respectful in listening to other beliefs and cultural views that are present (Gupta, 2011). Nonprofit organizations should contemplate the five identified themes from this study to ascertain whether any factors in the development of social, cultural, and perceptual barriers within their nonprofit organization exist. If so, leaders could focus on a process of bringing change to the culture. For this to happen, leadership must reassess the vision, mission, and goals being evidently displayed within the organization. Likewise, the foundation of leadership is to give sacrificially through knowledge, understanding, and transparency (Chen et al., 2014). The leader as a servant has a responsibility, which is serving the needs of all, without hesitation, biases, discrimination, or preferences. (Doh & Quigley, 2014).

The information revealed within this study unties a new avenue of research. Therefore, the opportunities and recommendations for future research are essentially limitless. Having a constant conversation between Christian ministry leaders may bridge the gap between nonprofit organizations and the social, cultural, and perceptual barriers female Christian ministry leaders face. Christian ministry leaders of nonprofit organizations may find substantial sustenance from reading this research as they carefully examine the behaviors of their organizations. Women in various leadership positions have learned to adapt and adopt too many of the social and cultural perceptions. Their behaviors have also challenged the set traditions and rituals by going beyond the norm through reaching for what they are purposed to do (Paustian-Underdahl et al., 2014).

Conclusions

Explored in the current qualitative study with a case study design were the perceptions and experiences of female Christian ministry leaders regarding barriers in nonprofit organizations. The theoretical framework used for this study was Servant leadership and inclusive leadership theory. Servant-leadership is a theoretical framework that advocates a leader's primary motivation and role as service to others (Greenleaf, 1977). Inclusive leadership is the practice of leadership that carefully includes the contributions of all stakeholders in the community or organization. Inclusion means being at the table at all levels of the organization, being a valued contributor and being fully responsible for your contribution to the ultimate result (Fierke et al., 2014).

Discussed in the extensive literature reviewed were the leadership disparities existed for women leaders in Christian ministry for nonprofit organizations. Five themes emerged from the current study interviews. Participants for the study revealed that female Christian ministry leaders do experience barriers. The majority of the participants revealed that the internal and external barriers do exist and have an emotional, mental, psychological, physical, and spiritual effect.

Prior to the current study, limited research was available on perceptions of the experiences that women leaders face in Christian ministry in nonprofit organizations. The purpose of this study is to explore how and why women leaders in Christian ministry explain the social, cultural, and perceptual barriers that affect them. The overall review examined the phenomenon of how women in leadership perceived their experiences as leaders, how they explained their own learned and inherent characteristics, why they persevered in the profession, and how they contended with barriers in Christian ministry. The study is centered on two relevant themes; to determine the barriers of female Christian ministry leaders: (a) reveal the personal, social, and perceptual barriers that women face, when they seek Christian leadership positions, (b) examine what measures women have taken to overcome these barriers, and (c) identify the inherent and learned characteristics necessary for Christian leadership, as it relates to the phenomenon of female Christian ministry leaders.

Revealed in the data were the personal, social, and perceptual barriers that women face when they seek Christian leadership positions and what some have done to overcome these barriers. It also identified the inherent and learned characteristics necessary for Christian leadership.

Therefore, this study provided insight on these barriers, and recommendations can be made so that women in leadership can be successful despite the barriers. Future study should be conducted for determining the impact that barriers have on female Christian ministry leaders, how many women have quit, disobeyed God, and are suffering from facing internal barriers due to the constraints.

References

Andronoviene, L. (2013). Leadership as a virtuous practice: Reflections on women and stained-glass ceilings. *Baptistic Theologies, 5*(1), 119-132.

Arvey, R. D., Zhang, Z., Avolio, B. J., & Krueger, R. F. (2007). Developmental and genetic determinants of leadership role occupancy among women. *Journal of Applied Psychology, 92*(3), 693–706.

Bacha, E., & Walker, S. (2013). The relationship between transformational leadership and followers' perceptions of fairness. *Journal of Business Ethics, 116*(3), 667-680. doi:10.1007/s10551-012-1507-z

Beaty, L., & Davis, T. J. (2012). Gender disparity in professional city management: making the case for enhancing leadership curriculum. *Journal of Public Affairs Education, 18*(4), 617-632.

Bennis, W., & Nanus, B. (1985) *"Leaders: The Strategies for Taking Charge"*. New York, Harper & Row.

Bennis, W.G. (2007). The challenges of leadership in the modem world—introduction to the special issue. *American Psychologist, 62*, 2–5.

Benson, J. D. (2015). *Motivation, productivity, and change management. Research starters:* Business (Online Edition).

Berger, T. A. (2014). Servant Leadership 2.0: A call for strong theory. *Sociological Viewpoints, 30*(1), 146-167.

Bono, J.E., & Judge, T.A. (2004). Personality and transformational and transactional leadership: A meta-analysis. *Journal of Applied Psychology, 89*, 901–910.

Bosch, D. J. (1993). *Transforming mission: Paradigm shifts in theology of mission.* Maryknoll, NY: Orbis Books.

Bowles, H. (2014). Review of women and executive office: Pathways and performance. *Administrative Science*

Quarterly 59 (4). Retrieved from NP39-NP41 PsycINFO, BSCOhost

Bryant-Anderson, R., & Roby, P. A. (2012). The experience of leadership: women and men shop stewards' perspectives in ten trade unions. *Labor Studies Journal, 37*(3), 271-292. doi:10.1177/0160449X12453771

Bush Jr., J. E. (2012). Dynamic diversity: Building class, age, race and gender in the church. *Pacifica, 25*(2), 202-203.

Cairney, P., & St Denny, E. (2015). Reviews of what is qualitative research and what is qualitative interviewing. *International Journal of Social Research Methodology: Theory & Practice, 18*(1), 117-125. doi:10.1080/13645579.2014.957434

Carson, D. A. (2012). *The intolerance of tolerance.* Grand Rapids, MI: Wm. B. Eerdmans.

Chau, S. (2011). An anatomy of corporate governance. *IUP Journal of Corporate Governance, 10*(1), 7-21.

Retrieved from
jttp://library.gcu.edu:2048/login?url=http://search.pr
oquest.com/docview/846781681

Chen, Z., Zhu, J., & Zhou, M. (2014). How does a servant leader fuel the service fire? A multilevel model of servant leadership, individual self-identity, group competition climate and customer service performance. *Journal of Applied Psychology, 100*(2). doi:10.1037/a0038036

Chin, J. L., & Sanchez-Hucles, J. (2007). Diversity and leadership. *American Psychologist, 62*(6), 608-609. doi:10.1037/0003-066X62.6.608

Christian, B. M., & Zippay, C. (2012). Breaking the yoke of racism & cultural biases. *Multicultural Education, 19*(4), 33-40.

Chung, Y. S. (2011). Why servant leadership? Its uniqueness and principles in the life of Jesus. *Journal of Asia Adventist Seminary, 14*(2), 159-170.

Cook, A. (2010). The denied calling: A look at the role of women in the Southern Baptist church. *Logos: A Journal of Undergraduate Research*, 3 189-205.

Cronin, C. (2014). Using case study research as a rigorous form of inquiry. *Nurse Researcher, 21*(5), 19-27 9p. doi:10.7748/nr.21.5.19. e1240

Crowley, E. D. (2014). 'Using new eyes': Photography as a spiritual practice for faith formation and worship. *Dialog: A Journal of Theology, 53*(1), 30-40. oi:10.1111/dial.12086

Dahlvig, J. E., & Longman, K. A. (2010). Women's leadership development: A study of defining moments. *Christian Higher Education, 9*(3), 238-258. doi:10.1080/15363750903182177

Doh, J. P., & Quigley, N. R. (2014). Responsible leadership and stakeholder management: Influence pathways and organizational outcomes. *Academy of Management Perspectives, 28*(3), 255-274.

Donaldson, T. (1996, September/October). Values in tension: Ethics away from home. Harvard Business Review, 74(5), 48-62. Church. Logos: *A Journal of Undergraduate Research,* 3189-205.

Duncan, C., & Schoor, M. (2015). Talking across boundaries: A case study of distributed governance. Voluntas: *International Journal of Voluntary & Nonprofit Organizations, 26*(3), 731-755. doi:10.1007/s11266-014-9453-2

Dzubinski, L. M. (2012). Gender diversity in mission work and leadership: Moving towards kingdom transformation. *Evangelical Review of Theology, 36*(4), 332-346.

England, T. D. (2011). The evolving self: a model of transformative leadership training utilizing the concept of mentoring for the ministry context. *The Journal of Applied Christian Leadership, 5*(2), 117.

Fiedler, M. (2010). Women as religious leaders: Breaking through the stained glass ceiling. *Huffington Post.*

Retrieved from http://www.huffingtonpost.com/maureen-fiedler/women-religious-leaders_b_766006.html

Fierke, K. K.; Lui, K. W.; Lepp, G. A.; & Baldwin, A. J. (2014). Teaching inclusive leadership through student-centered practices. *Journal of the Academy of Business Education, 15,* 51-65.

Fifer, J. J. (2015). Linking price transparency and organizational viability. *Hfm (Healthcare Financial Management), 69*(12), 30-30 1p.

Forbes (2011). *Impact 30.* Forbes. Retrieved from: http://www.forbes.com/impact-30/list.html

Frost, N. (2011). *Qualitative research methods in psychology: Combining core Approaches.* Berkshire, England: McGraw-Hill.

Gabarro, J. J. (1987). *The dynamics of taking charge.* Boston, MA: Harvard Business School Press.

Greenleaf, R.K. (1977). *Servant leadership: A journey into the nature of legitimate power & greatness.* New York, NY: Paulist Press

GuideStar (2011). 2011 *GuideStar Nonprofit Compensation Report.* Retrieved from http://www.guidestar.org/rxg/products/nonprofit-compensation-solutions/guidestar-nonprofit-compensationreport.aspx

Gupta, P. (2011). Leading innovation change - The Kotter way. *International Journal of Innovation Science, 3*(3), 141-150.

Haddad, M. (2013a). Diversity Works. *Mutuality, 20*(3), 22.

Haddad, M. (2013b). Encouraging and Equipping Female Leaders. *Mutuality, 20*(2), 20.

Herrera, R.; Duncan, P.; Green, M.; & Skaggs, S. (2012). The effect of gender on leadership and culture. Retrieved from *Global Business &*

Organizational Excellence 31(2), 7-48. *Business Source Complete*, EBSCO*host*

Holst, E., & Kirsch, A. (2015). Financial sector: Share of women in top decision-making bodies remains low. *DIW Economic Bulletin, 5*(4), 49-58.

Hong, S. (2012). Reversing a downward spiral: strengthening the church's community, holiness, and unity through intentional discipleship. *Asian Journal of Pentecostal Studies, 15*(1).

Isaacs, A. N. (2014). An overview of qualitative research methodology for public health researchers. *International Journal of Medicine & Public Health, 4*(4), 318-323. doi:10.4103/2230-8598.144055

Jaworski, J. (2012). Renewing leaders: Beyond servant leadership. *Reflections, 12*(1), 44-51.

Jenkins, S. (2014). John R. Wooden, Stephen R. Covey, and Servant leadership. *International Journal of Sports Science & Coaching, 9*(1), 1-24.

Johns, M. L. (2013). Breaking the glass ceiling: Structural, cultural, and organizational barriers preventing women from achieving senior and Executive Positions. *Perspectives in Health Information Management*, 1-11.

Johnson, B., & Christensen, L.B. (2012). *Educational research: Quantitative, qualitative, and mixed approaches*. Los Angeles, CA: Sage.

Kaufmann, F. A., Harrel, G., Milam, C. P., Woolverton, N., & Miller, J. (1986). The nature, role, and influence of mentors in the lives of gifted adults. *Journal of Counseling & Development, 64*(9), 576.

Kemp, I. S. (2016). The blessing, power, and authority of the church. *Evangelical Review of Theology, 40*(2), 128-139.

Kessler, V. (2013). Pitfalls in 'biblical' leadership. *Verbum Et Ecclesia, 34*(1), 1-7. doi:10.4102/ve.v34i1.721

Klenke, K., Wallace, J. R., & Martin, S. M. (2015). *Qualitative research in the study of leadership*.

United Kingdom: Emerald Group Publishing Limited.

Kohl, M. W. (2006). Radical transformation in preparation for the ministry. *International Congregational Journal*, 6(1), 39-51.

Koshal, J.O. (2005). Servant leadership theory: Application of the construct of service in the context of Kenyan leaders and managers. *Paper presented at the Servant Leadership Research Roundtable, Regent University, School of Leadership.* Retrieved from http://www.regent.edu/acad/global/publications/sl_proceedings/home.shtml

Lambert, V. A., & Lambert, C. E. (2012). Editorial: Qualitative Descriptive Research: An Acceptable Design. *Pacific Rim International Journal of Nursing Research*, 16(4), 255-256.

Marianne, D., & Miemie, S. (2014). Perceptions of factors influencing the career success of professional and business women in South Africa. *South African*

Journal of Economic and Management Sciences, (5), 531

Marsh, C. (2013). Business executives' perceptions of ethical leadership and its development. *Journal of Business Ethics, 114*(3), 565-582. doi:10.1007/s10551-012-1366-7

Marshall, J. (2008). Ethics for the real world: Creating a personal code to guide decisions in work and life. *Financial Executive, 24*(7), 18.

Mayring, Philipp (2000). Qualitative Content Analysis [28 paragraphs]. *Forum Qualitative Sozialforschung / Forum: Qualitative Social Research, 1*(2), Art. 20, http://nbn-resolving.de/urn:nbn:de:0114-fqs0002204.

McBride, A. (2011). Lifting the barriers? Workplace education and training, Women and Job Progression. *Gender, Work & Organization, 18*(5), 528-547. doi:10.1111/j.1468-0432.2011.00574.x

McLeskey, J., & Waldron, N. (n.d). Effective leadership makes schools truly inclusive. *Phi Delta Kappan, 96*(5), 68-73.

Mento, M. (2014). Lack of women in top roles hinders nonprofits, female nonprofit workers. (2014). *Chronicle of Philanthropy, 21*(22), 4. Retrieved from Academic Search Premier Database.

Merriam, S. B. (2009). *Qualitative research: A guide to design and implementation.* San Francisco, California: Jossey-Bass, 2009.

Meyer, D. A. (2010). Why go to church? *Concordia Journal,* 36(2), 89-96.

Michailidis, M. P., Morphitou, R. N., & Theophylatou, I. (2012). Women at work equality versus inequality: Barriers for advancing in the workplace. *International Journal of Human Resource Management, 23*(20), 4231-4245. doi:10.1080/09585192.2012.665071

Mock, M. S. (2005). Confined by the stained-glass ceiling. *The Chronicle of Higher Education, 52*(11), B.24

Moor, A., Cohen, A., & Beeri, O. (2015). In quest of excellence, not power: Women's paths to positions of influence and leadership. *Advancing women in leadership*, 351-11.

Moustakas, C. (1994). *Phenomenological research methods.* Thousand Oaks, CA: Sage Publications.

Newkirk, D., & Cooper, B. S. (2013). Preparing women for Baptist church leadership: Mentoring impact on beliefs and practices of female ministers. *Journal of Research on Christian Education, 22*(3), 323-343. doi:10.1080/10656219.2013.845120

Noland, R. (2009). From neutrino worship to real transformation. *Common Ground Journal, 7*(1), 60-70.

Northouse, P.G., (2007). *Leadership theory and practice (4th ed.)* Thousand Oaks, CA: Sage Publications.

Ng KY, Ang S, Chan KY. (2008). Personality and leader effectiveness: A moderated mediation model of leadership self-efficacy, job demands, and job autonomy. *Journal of Applied Psychology, 93*, 733–743.

Nwoye, M. I. (2011). Perspectives on entrepreneurial leadership: Obstacles delimiting women. *Pakistan Journal of Women's Studies = Alam-e-Niswan = Alam-i Nisvan, 18*(2), 65-76.

Ochoa, G. (2011). Women in leadership for a democratic society. *Americas, 63*(3), 48-49.

Ott, U. F. (2011). The Influence of Cultural Activity Types on Buyer-Seller Negotiations: A Game Theoretical Framework for Intercultural Negotiations. *International Negotiation, 16*(3), 427-450. doi:10.1163/157180611X592941

Paustian-Underdahl, S. C., Walker, L. S., & Woehr, D. J. (2014). Gender and perceptions of leadership effectiveness: A meta-analysis of contextual moderators. *Journal of Applied Psychology*, *99*(6), 1129-1145. doi:10.1037/a0036751

Pearce, C.L., Conger JA. (2003). *Shared leadership: Reframing the hows and whys of leadership.* Thousand Oaks: Sage.

Pringle, J., Hendry, C., & McLafferty, E. (2011). Phenomenological approaches: challenges and choices. *Nurse Researcher, 18*(2), 7-18.

Rabinovich, M., & Kacen, L. (2013). Qualitative coding methodology for interpersonal study. *Psychoanalytic Psychology, 30*(2), 210-231. doi:10.1037/a0030897

Ragins, B. R., Townsend, B., & Mattis, M. (1998). Gender gap in the executive suite: CEOs and female executives report on breaking the glass ceiling. *Academy of Management Executive, 12,* 28–42.

Rivkin, W., Diestel, S., & Schmidt, K. (2014). The positive relationship between servant leadership and employees' psychological health: A multi-method

approach. *Zeitschrift für Personalforschung,*
28(1/2), 52-72. doi:10.1688/ZfP-2014-01-Rivkin
doi:10.1260/1747-9541.9.1.37

Rogers, M. (2010). A dangerous idea? Martin Luther, E. Y. Mullins, and the priesthood of all believers. *Westminster Theological Journal, 72*(1), 119-134.

Romani, L., & Szkudlarek, B. (2014). The struggles of the interculturalists: Professional ethical identity and early stages of codes of ethics development. *Journal of Business Ethics, 119*(2), 173-191. doi:10.1007/s10551-012-1610-1

Ross, C. 2015. Often, Often, Often Goes the Christ in the Stranger's Guise: Hospitality as a Hallmark of Christian Ministry. *International Bulletin of Missionary Research 39*, (4), 175-179. Retrieved from ATLA Religion Database with ATLASerials, EBSCOhost.

Ruiz-Jiménez, J. M., & Fuentes-Fuentes, M. M. (2016). Management capabilities, innovation and gender diversity in the top management team: An empirical analysis in technology-based SMEs. *Business Research Quarterly, 19*(2), 107-121. doi: 10.1016/j.brq.2015.08.003

Ryan, M. K., Haslam, S. A., Hersby, M. D., & Bongiorno, R. (2011). Think crisis–think female: The glass cliff and contextual variation in the think manager–think male stereotype. *Journal of Applied Psychology, 96*(3), 470-484. doi:10.1037/a0022133

Sawyer, K. R. (2016). True church, national church, minority church: Episcopacy and authority in the restored church of Ireland. *Church History, 85*(2), 219-245. doi:10.1017/S0009640716000408

Scott, H. G. (2010). Desiring the kingdom: Worship, worldview, and cultural formation. *Christian Education Journal, 7*(1), 236-239.

Singh, K. D. (2015). Creating your own qualitative research approach: Selecting, integrating and operationalizing philosophy, methodology, and methods. *Vision* (09722629), *19*(2), 132-146. doi:10.1177/0972262915575657

Skelly, J. J., & Johnson, J. B. (2011). Glass ceilings and great expectations: Gender stereotype impact on female professionals. *Southern Law Journal, 21*(1), 59-70. Retrieved from http://search.proquest.com/docview/1173814495?accountid=7374

Smith, P., Crittenden, N., & Caputi, P. (2012). Measuring women's beliefs about glass ceilings: Development of the career pathways survey. *Gender in Management, 27*(2), 68-80. doi:http://dx.doi.org/10.1108/17542411211214130

Stake R. E. (1998) Case studies. In: Denzin N. K, Lincoln Y. S, editors. *Strategies of qualitative inquiry*. Thousand Oaks, CA: Sage. pp. 86–109.

Stake R. E. (1978) The case study method in social inquiry. *Educational Researcher.* 7(2):5–8.

Stake R. E. (1995) *The art of case study research.* Thousand Oaks, CA: Sage;

Ştefan, R. (2008). Christian ethics and the ethics of contemporary man. *HEC Forum, 20*(1), 61-73. doi:10.1007/s10730-008-9064-7

Stob, G. (1968). Free responsibility in the church. *Reformed Journal, 18*(8), 5-8.

Suk Bong, C., Thi Bich Hanh, T., & Byung IL, P. (2015). Inclusive leadership and work engagement: Mediating roles of affective organizational commitment and creativity. *Social Behavior & Personality: An International Journal, 43*(6), 931-943.

Swinth, Y., Tomlin, G., & Luthman, M. (2015). Content analysis of qualitative research on children and youth with Autism, 1993-2011: Considerations for occupational therapy services. *American Journal of Occupational*

Therapy, *69*(5), p1-p9 9p. doi:10.5014/ajot.2015.017970

Taylor, S. G., & Pattie, M. W. (2014). When does ethical leadership affect workplace incivility? The moderating role of follower personality. *Business Ethics Quarterly*, *24*(4), 595-616. doi:10.5840/beq201492618

Thomas, I. (2014). Revitalizing the women's ministry: Women mentoring to the women a Titus 2 project. (Order No. 3611947, Liberty University). *ProQuest Dissertations and Theses,* 167. Retrieved from http://search.proquest.com/docview/1504845465?accountid=7374. (1504845465).

Tidball, D. (2012). Leaders as servants: A resolution of the tension. *Evangelical Review of Theology, 36*(1), 31-47.

Valk, J. (2010). Leadership for transformation: The impact of a Christian worldview. *Journal of Leadership Studies, 4*(3), 83-86. doi:10.1002/jls.20183

Vasavada, T. (2012). A cultural feminist perspective on leadership in nonprofit organizations: A case of women leaders in India. *Public Administration Quarterly, 36*(4), 462-503.

Vevere, V. (2014). Ethical leadership: student perceptions of exercising ethical influence in organization. *European Integration Studies, 8,* 159-167. doi: 10.5755/j01.eis.0.8.6987

Virick, M., & Greer, C. R. (2012). Gender diversity in leadership succession: Preparing for the future. *Human Resource Management, 51*(4), 575-600. doi:10.1002/hrm.21487

Vogel, J., & Finkelstein, S. (2011). Attracting Great Mentors: Seven strategies to cultivate. *OD Practitioner, 43*(3), 18-24.

Washington, C. E. (2010). Mentoring, organizational rank, and women's perceptions of advancement opportunities in the workplace. *Forum on Public Policy Online*, 2010, 2.

Wienclaw, R. A. (2015). Gender and domestic responsibilities. *Research Starters: Sociology* (Online Edition)

Yancey, G. (1999). An examination of effects: Residential and church integration upon racial attitudes of whites. *Sociological Perspectives 42,* 279–304.

Yin R. K (1999). Enhancing the quality of case studies in health services research. *Health Services Research. 34*(5 Pt 2):1209–1224.

Yin R. K. (2009). *Case study research: Design and methods*. 4th ed. Thousand Oaks, CA: Sage.

Yin R. K. (2012) *Applications of case study research*. 3rd ed. Thousand Oaks, CA: Sage; 2012.

www.ingramcontent.com/pod-product-compliance
Lightning Source LLC
Chambersburg PA
CBHW021958160426
43197CB00007B/174